THE ART AND HUMOR OF JOHN TREVER

The Art and Humor of JOHN TREVER

FIFTY YEARS OF POLITICAL CARTOONING

JOHN TREVER

UNIVERSITY OF NEW MEXICO PRESS ~ ALBUQUERQUE

ISBN 978-0-8263-6239-1 (paper)
ISBN 978-0-8263-6240-7 (electronic)

Library of Congress Control Number: 2021930603

Cover illustration courtesy of John Trever
Designed by Felicia Cedillos
Composed in Melior LT Std 11.5/16.5

Contents

Introduction

When I retired from full-time editorial cartooning for the *Albuquerque Journal* in 2010, I anticipated slowly fading away, like MacArthur's generals. But, as an India ink–stained wretch, the fading away has taken a bit longer than I expected. I had donated thousands of my original cartoons to the Center for Southwest Research at the University of New Mexico, and, with a start on clearing out my office, was happily minding my own business (well, okay, I was minding New Mexico's business, too, since I was still doing a local cartoon for the *Sunday Journal*), when the interim director for UNM Press, Richard Schuetz, approached me about publishing a new book that would include recent cartoons but more importantly a narrative about the evolution of my career, my experiences at the *Journal*, and some insights into the craft of political cartooning.

I was intrigued by the project, since my three previous books, produced by the Albuquerque Publishing Company, had been collections of several hundred cartoons with little text except for a line or two of context with each cartoon. With the encouragement of the *Journal*'s publisher, Bill Lang, and Stephen Hull, the new director of UNM Press, I submitted a proposal for a book of my cartoons interspersed with personal history and a look at the business and techniques involved in what has been the thriving field of newspaper cartooning but is now somewhat threatened by changes in the media world. Meanwhile, as the proposal was being considered and duly accepted by UNM Press, I had been invited by Albuquerque's Oasis continuing education program to give a couple of lectures about my cartooning career and the nature of humor in editorial cartooning, which ended up providing the framework for this book.

The result is the volume you now have before you, for which I have many people to thank. In addition to Bill Lang, Richard Schuetz, and Stephen Hull, for their backing and guidance, I would like to acknowledge the patient assistance of my editor at the press, James Ayers, and other members of the staff—Felicia Cedillos, Sonia Dickey, Alexandra Hoff, Stacy Lunsford, and Katherine White—for their contributions to the success of this project. Thanks also go to Kathleen Raskob and the crew at Oasis for their part in inspiring this narrative.

I must also acknowledge my colleagues at the *Journal* for their decades of journalistic dedication (their stories were the basis for so much of my work), along with the tolerance and counsel of my editors over the years—Jerry Crawford, Eric McCrossen, Bill Hume, Kent Walz, Karen Moses, Steve Mills, Dan Herrera, and D'Val Westphal. I am likewise grateful for the enthusiastic support by Mary Ann Weems and the Weems Gallery.

Finally, I am indebted to my parents, the late John C. and Elizabeth Trever, for encouraging and assisting me in following my dreams, and to my wife Karen and our family, for years of patient understanding and support for the long hours spent in creating these drawings and this book.

JOHN TREVER
Albuquerque
November, 2020

1. Portfolio

Cartooning is a non-credentialed profession. There is no established career path to becoming an editorial cartoonist. It doesn't require a college degree. You don't need to graduate from an accredited Cartoon School. There are no cartoon orals or a cartoon thesis to write and defend. Nor are there cartoon boards or a cartoon bar exam to pass. You don't need a state cartoon license to practice cartooning. And while there are cartoonist professional associations, they are not in the business of enforcing standards to limit entry to, and competition in, the business. All that is really needed is a portfolio of one's work . . . and an editor who is able to judge whether or not you can do the job. Like an actor's or musician's audition, the portfolio will quickly reflect your level of talent and experience. The fact that the editor doesn't really need to look at a résumé but can simply glance through your portfolio is thus a great advantage. Or a disadvantage, if the portfolio doesn't measure up to what that editor is looking for. In the case of editorial cartooning, of course, it also helps if your political views are not totally at variance with the editor's.

In the fall of 1976 I had taken my portfolio to New Mexico and the offices of the *Albuquerque Journal*. I had mailed my résumé and some sample cartoons in response to their ad for a cartoonist in *Editor & Publisher* and had flown down from Denver for an interview. My large, zip-up portfolio case contained examples of work done for the *Sentinel Newspapers*, a group of fourteen suburban weeklies in the Denver area. For the previous four years, since leaving the Air Force, I had been doing all their editorial artwork: illustrations, caricatures, maps, column head designs, cover drawings, as well as several political cartoons per week. The job at the *Journal* would consist of similar duties, so I included several large illustrations as well as cartoons and caricatures in my portfolio.

I didn't realize it at the time, but if I got hired, I would be part of the editorial board of the *Journal*, so I was interviewed not only by the editorial-page editor but also by the editor, senior editor, and managing editor. My portfolio apparently passed muster, but there would be two more challenges. First, they all took me to lunch in a rambling adobe restaurant in Albuquerque's historic Old Town. Having been raised by a Swedish mom on a meat-and-potatoes diet that rarely saw any spices beyond salt and pepper, and despite four years in Denver, I was a novice when it came to New Mexican fare with its signature red or green chile. Visions of "Montezuma's Revenge" came to mind as I perused the extensive menu. I don't remember now, but I imagine I ordered tacos or a burrito platter—with the mild "tourista" chile, thank you.

Having managed to survive lunch, I was tasked with a second challenge. As I was preparing to return to the airport to fly home, I was given several photos. They wished to see how I would caricature some leading New Mexico politicians: Governor Jerry Apodaca, US Senator Joseph Montoya, and Albuquerque mayor Harry Kinney. After flying back to Denver, I quickly tackled that assignment and mailed my efforts back.

Apparently the caricatures were recognizable enough (although the governor's sketch could use some work, I was told), because shortly thereafter I received a call from the *Journal*'s managing editor, Frankie McCarty, offering me the job. With understandable excitement I announced to my wife, Susan, as well as our two-year-old Alan and month-old Andy, that we were headed south!

The next two months were a blur. We quickly arranged to put our house, which we'd bought only ten months earlier, on the market. We all drove down to Albuquerque and found a house to rent, then we returned to Denver to pack while I continued to draw for the *Sentinels* for the next two weeks. My *Sentinel* editors seemed reluctant to see me go, and I had mixed feelings, too. Many of my colleagues there were in their first journalism job out of college, and we were a close-knit group. Of course, many were also eager to graduate to daily newspapers, and several would leave within a year or two after my departure to work for large metropolitan papers. The editors even invited me to help choose my replacement, who turned out to be a fellow Syracuse University graduate.

With the 1976 general election rapidly approaching, the *Journal* had hoped to have some local cartoons before election day. So back I went to Albuquerque, and, staying at a nearby motel a couple of blocks from the *Journal*'s offices, I spent two days of in-processing and shopping for art materials, and the rest of the week I concentrated on turning out editorial cartoons. The major statewide race was between New Mexico's senior senator, Joe Montoya, and GOP challenger Jack Schmitt, a former astronaut who had travelled to the moon on Apollo 17. Montoya had gotten some criticism when he tried to belittle Schmitt by comparing him to a NASA "space monkey." So my inaugural cartoon for the *Journal* depicted Montoya as a big game hunter.

The following day's cartoon featured Bob Dole, President Gerald Ford's running mate, who was paying a last-minute visit to New Mexico in hopes of winning the state for the Republican ticket. Then, stumped for a Sunday topic the next day, I finally settled on another Montoya cartoon, but this gave the editors pause, even though they had endorsed Schmitt earlier. They typically eschewed partisan commentary the Sunday before an election, preferring to merely summarize their endorsements. But they decided to run the cartoon, which was an early indication of the great editorial freedom I would enjoy with the *Journal.*

That weekend, with our Denver home sold, we moved our young family to Albuquerque and began settling into our new life in the Land of Enchantment. For the first thirty-three years of my life I had moved every four or five years. New Mexico would be my home for the next forty-five (and counting).

2. Pogo

While there may be no prescribed route to a career in political cartooning, it must certainly begin with falling in love with cartoons and comics. In my case, it was the discovery of the comic strip *Pogo* that started me on a long, circuitous journey to becoming an editorial cartoonist. In 1953 we were living outside Chicago, where my father, Dr. John C. Trever, a key figure in bringing the Dead Sea Scrolls to the world's attention, was working for the National Council of Churches. While he traveled around the country promoting the new Revised Standard Version of the bible, I was enjoying a typical 1950s suburban childhood: riding my bike, playing baseball, swapping bubble-gum cards with the kids on the block, running my Lionel train set, joining the Cub Scouts, listening to the Lone Ranger, Sergeant Preston, and Jack Benny on the radio, and developing an unfortunate devotion to the Chicago Cubs.

I had also developed a taste for drawing, particularly sketches of trains. A branch line of the Chicago & Northwestern Railroad, still using steam engines at that time, ran within a hundred yards of our house, and I liked to sit in my upstairs bedroom window and draw the freight trains that rumbled by. Meanwhile, I'd discovered comic books, in particular the Walt Disney comics, and I was also an avid reader of the comic strips in the newspaper delivered to our home. Chicago had something like six newspapers back then, but the paper our family took didn't run *Pogo*. However, my best friend's family, two doors down, did have *Pogo* in their paper, and it was at their house, in the back pages of the *Chicago Daily News*, that I found this delightful comic strip, drawn by Walt Kelly, a former Disney artist. His unique cast of animal characters, based in Georgia's Okefenokee Swamp, featured superb artwork and amusing, Southern-vernacular dialogue as well as some subtle political commentary, which, as a nine-year-old, I didn't yet appreciate.

Poor Mrs. Carrigan. I hounded her to let me clip out the *Pogo* strips from back issues stacked in her basement. These I saved and soon began pasting into a scrapbook. When our family moved to West Virginia a couple of years later, I lobbied for subscribing to the local paper that ran *Pogo*, the *Charleston Daily Mail*. I continued to religiously save the strips and paste them into a growing group of scrapbooks. When I discovered that there were also *Pogo* comic books as well as annual volumes of selected *Pogo* strips, I began adding those to my collection.

In early 1957, when I was thirteen, the *Daily Mail* announced a contest sponsored by the Newspaper Comics Council to draw your favorite comics character and write an essay on "What Newspaper Comics Mean to Me" in the classic one hundred words or less. I had no trouble deciding on which comic strip to feature in my entry. With my art materials spread out on the dining-room table, I carefully copied (not traced!) a cartoon of Pogo Possum and Albert Alligator from the back of Walt Kelly's *I Go Pogo* book on a sheet of typewriter paper. On another sheet I typed out a few thoughts on the comics in my best adolescent prose, then I sent my entry downtown to the *Daily Mail's* offices.

In mid-February I learned that my entry had taken first place in the state, and then, just a week later, that I'd won the national first prize! The very next weekend Mom and I flew to New York and were ensconced in the Waldorf-Astoria. I was to participate in a whirlwind weekend helping to publicize Newspaper Comics Week. This included appearing on several TV and radio shows, receiving front-row seats for a Broadway performance of "Li'l Abner," changing the Times Square street sign to "Newspaper

My contest drawing of Pogo.

Comics Square," and meeting Walt Kelly and having lunch with him at the Penthouse Club overlooking Central Park. At the time it was all a bit overwhelming for a thirteen-year-old, but the experience obviously had a big influence on the course of my future career.

A few months after this, Kelly sent us a couple of original *Pogo* strips, along with all of his annual books up to that point. For several years we would receive a Christmas card from the Kellys, which usually featured his parody of "Deck the Halls." Sadly, he passed away in 1973. I have maintained a *Pogo* collection of sorts, including all the books, the Dell comics, a few original strips, some of the books reprinting his earliest strips, and other memorabilia. To this day, in homage to Walt Kelly, I often imitate his practice of outlining the strip panels by hand with occasional small flourishes instead of drawing straight lines with a ruling pen.

Mom and I meet with Walt Kelly in New York.

Another part of my prize would be a correspondence course in cartooning from the Famous Artists Schools in Connecticut: twenty-four lessons in everything from basic cartoon-drawing techniques to how to develop a comic strip. Several well-known cartoonists, including Rube Goldberg, Milton Caniff, and Al Capp, lent their names to this enterprise, but the lessons would be critiqued by the school's staff members. Upon my sixteenth birthday I received my course lessons, bound in three large loose-leaf notebooks. The course was to be completed in three years, and I kept on schedule through my last two years of high school. But progress slowed during four years of college, and the last few lessons weren't done until I was about to graduate.

I was still very busy cartooning during college, however. From my first days as a freshman at Syracuse University until I graduated four years later, I drew a gag panel, which came to be titled *Trever on Campus*, for the student newspaper, the *Daily Orange*. It ran on the editorial page, but it didn't deal with politics. It focused instead on the foibles of campus life: classes, cafeteria food, studying or the lack of it, dating, parties, fraternities and sororities, sports, and so on. The early sixties were still the "Joe College / Suzy Coed" years, just before the campus was impacted by the Vietnam War, the draft, and the civil-rights movement, when college was still largely an escape from the real world.

"Some of you may be under the impression that this course is not particularly difficult . . ."

A "Trever on Campus" in the *Daily Orange.*

This daily cartooning was a great proving ground. I learned to meet regular deadlines, received feedback from fellow students, finding what did and did not work, and began developing a drawing style of my own. During the spring semester of my senior year, I collected some of my favorite cartoons into a small book that I composed and pasted up myself in the basement studios of the just-completed Newhouse School of Public Communications. I engaged a local company to print several hundred copies, which I then sold around campus.

The previous August, President Lyndon Johnson had come to Syracuse for the dedication of the Newhouse School, at which time he'd announced the Tonkin Gulf incident and the subsequent escalation of our involvement in Vietnam. This was before the draft lottery was instituted, and many students were concerned about losing their deferments once they left school. Rather than apply for a newspaper job at one of the local Syracuse papers after graduating, as I'd anticipated, I began looking into graduate schools. I applied to Stanford and the University of Chicago to study political science. I had actually entered Syracuse as a math major, having been strongly influenced by the post-Sputnik emphasis on math and science (the first STEM push, if you will). But after some second-semester struggles with differential calculus, social sciences had suddenly looked more attractive. I also enjoyed English literature. Syracuse had an art school, and I began taking some classes there. By my junior year I was allowed to craft a combined major in literature, art, and political science. For a senior paper I scoured all the newspapers from around the country that I could find at the library and wrote about the political cartoons of the 1964 presidential campaign, with nary a thought that I would one day be doing them myself.

The University of Chicago offered me a generous fellowship in political science, so I started grad school in the fall of 1965 at their Gothic campus in the Hyde Park area of south Chicago. At this point I took a vacation from cartooning as I plunged into my poli-sci classes and roamed the seven-level stacks of the university library to do research for term papers. The U of C was a big change from Syracuse, particularly when it came to social life. The undergraduates were busy organizing antiwar protests, burning draft cards, and holding "teach-ins," but the graduate school seemed largely removed from all that as we pursued our studies (and the occasional visit to Rush Street or Wrigley Field).

During the summer of 1966 I returned my focus to cartooning. Staying at my brother's house near the University of Southern California, which he was attending (and from which both our parents had graduated), I worked on developing a comic strip. My previous freelance effort had been during the summer after my high school graduation, when I worked up a series of single-panel gag cartoon "roughs" to send off to magazines. At that time there were many magazines running cartoons, such as the *New Yorker*, *Collier's*, the *Saturday Evening Post*, *Look*, *Esquire*, *Playboy*, *Good Housekeeping*, and many more, but because I had subscribed to it,

My first cartoon in *Boy's Life*.

I chose *Boy's Life* to submit my first batch to. On my first try I sold three cartoons for the princely sum of twenty-five dollars each! A bit of beginner's luck, obviously, because after that I had no more sales the rest of the summer.

A comic strip would be more of a challenge to sell, as the competition is fierce and established artists have an advantage. I had noticed a trend toward "history" strips then, such as *B.C.*, *Hagar the Horrible* and *Wizard of Id*. I decided to try a humor strip with characters from ancient Greece. After obtaining several books on Greek history and civilization for reference, I set to work, finally producing three weeks of samples of strip I named *Homer*.

Not knowing much about newspaper syndicates, and not having a yet-to-be-invented scanner or even a Xerox machine at my disposal, when I returned home to Cleveland at the end of the summer, I delivered the bulky package of large original drawings in person to the Newspaper Enterprise Association, a syndicate conveniently located in Cleveland. A few weeks later they returned the package with a nice letter, but no sale.

Photostat of two "Homer" samples.

Finally, I managed to get the strips photostated and reduced so I could put them all in a 9×12" binder. This allowed me to mail out the strip samples to a succession of other syndicates while I pursued my second year of classes at Chicago. My reward was a growing collection of rejection letters.

But my life was about to take another turn. I received an offer to be an intern in the art department of the *Cleveland Plain Dealer* during the summer of 1967. This came from William Ware, executive editor of the "PD," whom I'd met at a Newspaper Comics Council function during my New York trip a decade earlier. I eagerly accepted, and in June I joined the "bullpen" of staff artists at the paper, which then numbered seven. In addition, the *Plain Dealer* had its own editorial cartoonist, a sports cartoonist, and a feature cartoonist, each with his own office.

At first my job largely consisted of photo retouching, and I learned to operate an air brush for the first time. Then I began to get a few assignments for illustrations and cartoons. My first drawing for the news pages was of black-power militant H. Rap Brown, and it was followed by numerous spot cartoons for news stories and columns, an occasional locator map, and regular sketches for the "Action Line" Q&A feature. Following the example of a fellow bullpen artist, I would clip out each of my published drawings to be pasted into a scrapbook.

To say I loved this job would be an understatement. Every day, as I rode the bus from my parents' suburban Cleveland home in Berea to the PD offices downtown, I looked forward to the camaraderie of the bullpen and the energy of a large metropolitan newspaper. These were the "hot lead" days of newspapering, with linotype and Ludlow machines, photoengraving, zinc plates, stereotyping, and Teletypes that spit out yellow sheets of wire copy.

I enjoyed newspaper-art

Examples of *Plain Dealer* sketches.

work so much, in fact, that I decided to forego the third year of my fellowship at Chicago and stay on as a regular employee at the *Plain Dealer*. As soon as I left school, however, my local draft board ended my deferment and began the process of inviting me into military service. During that fall and winter I received two "Greetings" letters from Uncle Sam and took my draft physical, but I managed to get two postponements while I pursued possible options for alternative service. I interviewed with several federal agencies in Washington and applied to the Peace Corps, but nothing would provide another deferment. Finally, having received a third and final draft notice, I bade farewell to the PD bullpen and enlisted in the US Air Force in early March of 1968.

My four-year military career was another detour away from cartooning, albeit an interesting and educational one. After officer training in San Antonio, I was commissioned as a second lieutenant and sent to F. E. Warren Air Force Base in Cheyenne, Wyoming, to become part of the Strategic Air Command's Minuteman missile force. This entailed pulling regular twenty-four-hour "alerts" as part of a two-man crew in one of the twenty missile-command centers scattered over southeast Wyoming, western Nebraska, and northeast Colorado. Each underground command center, or "capsule," was responsible for ten Minuteman nuclear missiles. Unlike earlier liquid-fueled missile systems, the Minuteman was solid-fueled and rarely needed maintenance. Most of my alerts were uneventful, interrupted only by the occasional routine message from headquarters or an alarm from a jackrabbit entering the security perimeter around one of the missile silos. Meals were brought down the elevator from the kitchen topside. We had no TV, but we had a lot of time for reading and studying (some of the crew members were in advanced-degree programs on base). We either drove to the launch-control facilities in motor-pool station wagons or flew in "Huey" helicopters to the more distant sites. Such was life on the front lines of nuclear deterrence in the Cold War. I have to admit, it was a high-paid babysitting job, albeit with a top-secret crypto clearance. I didn't envy my fellow missile officers in the Titan missile program, however. Theirs was a liquid-fueled missile, and each crew was assigned to a single missile. In 1980, as I was safely ensconced in my cartoonist's chair, a maintenance accident caused an explosion at one of Little Rock Air Force Base's Titan II silos, propelling the missile warhead some distance away. It didn't detonate—you would have heard about that—but I commemorated the incident with this cartoon:

"IF'N THIS HERE'S A EXAMPLE OF THE GUMMINT'S NEW TARGETIN' STRATEGY, I DON'T THINK MUCH OF IT...."

Back above ground, I studied the stock market, practiced my five-string banjo, fly-fished in some of Wyoming's mountain streams, and learned to ski in my spare time. Years later, sitting at coffee one day, some of my older colleagues at the *Albuquerque Journal* started telling war stories, with the edit-page editor recounting his Korean War hardships. When it came my turn, all I could think of was, "Well, there was the day I was out on alert and the oven-refrigerator unit broke down . . ."

While in Cheyenne I subscribed to the *Denver Post* and became a big fan of their political cartoonist Pat Oliphant, whose work I had discovered while researching my senior paper at Syracuse. He had moved from Australia, joining the *Post* in time for the 1964 election campaign. By 1968 he was a Pulitzer Prize winner and nationally syndicated. I was intrigued by his new and different style of political cartooning, often clipping out his cartoons and taping them up on the walls of my apartment. I began to realize that one could become syndicated not just with a comic strip, but also through editorial cartoons.

I completed my Air Force service in June of 1972 and moved to Denver in hopes of resuming a newspaper art career. I enrolled in a night class at a local art school to brush up on my commercial art skills. Neither of Denver's daily papers was hiring, but on a chance visit to an Aurora weekly newspaper's office, the helpful receptionist suggested I contact their main office. It turned out that most of Denver's suburban and community weeklies had been purchased the year before by the Minneapolis Star and Tribune Company, forming the *Sentinel Newspapers*. Luckily, they were hiring. Armed with my portfolio of four-year-old samples from my stint at the *Plain Dealer*, I interviewed at the central *Sentinel* office in north Denver. Their only artist was in the advertising department, but they had no artist on the editorial side.

I was offered a position in the editorial art department, which would consist of one person—me.

I went right to work in mid-July, handling any and all assignments that came my way from the fourteen newspapers in the group, including illustrations, spot cartoons, caricatures, maps, column-head designs, section-front drawings with one or two colors, and even a bit of courtroom sketching. As for editorial cartoons, normally I would do one for the network and as many others for the individual papers as the editors wanted and time permitted. The *Sentinels* were printed on Wednesday night and distributed on Thursday, so often I'd take Thursdays off and work Saturdays, particularly during ski season.

Initially I worked out of the Sentinel office in Englewood, one of the southern Denver suburbs. The staff here was responsible for several of the weeklies covering south Denver and nearby suburbs. It was a young and energetic group in a small space, but they managed to squeeze my drawing board in. We often socialized together after hours. One of my lasting memories there is watching the Watergate hearings in May 1973 on a portable TV set up in the newsroom. Below is a sample of my work at the time, taking off on the "streaking" fad.

By 1974 I was married to my girlfriend from Cheyenne and we had

"We finally convinced him it's the only way to prove he'd never be involved in a cover-up . . ."

a baby on the way. I had been transferred north to the Sentinel central offices, which housed the administrative, editorial, and advertising staff and was where the papers were printed. I enjoyed a bit more office space and became friends with the sports writers and photographers also located there. Susan and I moved to a nice duplex in central Denver near a bus line, so I would usually commute to work, affording me an opportunity to read the *Rocky Mountain News* each morning.

Other local publications had begun reprinting some of my Sentinel work, and I also provided cartoons to *Aspen Today*, a short-lived alternative to the long-established *Aspen Times*. In 1975 I began doing a weekly cartoon for the *Vail Trail*, like the one below featuring President Ford, who vacationed at Vail ski area.

One afternoon in 1975 I had a chance to visit Pat Oliphant at his *Denver Post* office. I quizzed him about his methods and got several tips, and we had a nice chat before he needed to begin inking his cartoon for the next day. I had been reluctant to bring any of my work to show him, but I promised some samples for him to critique at another visit. Unfortunately, a short time later he left the *Post* for the *Washington Star*, so I never got that opportunity.

I also met the chief political cartoonist for the Scripps-Howard newspapers, Gene Bassett, who had come to Denver to work out of the *Rocky Mountain News* office for a while. This time I did bring some samples along, and he graciously invited me to join the Association of American Editorial Cartoonists.

By 1976 my career at the Sentinels and my freelance work were both going very nicely, and I'd even received a few awards for my cartoons. But my ambition was still to work at a daily paper. At first I hoped to stay in Denver, as Susan and I had just bought our first house. The *Post* had already hired Mike Keefe to replace Oliphant, but the editor of the *Rocky Mountain News* had expressed some interest in my work. They had just hired a new editorial page

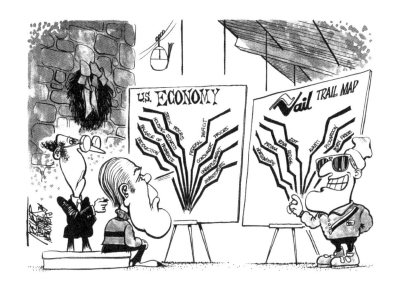

editor, however, and I gathered they couldn't afford to add a cartoonist until another year or so. A year or two later they did hire Ed Stein, who enjoyed a productive career there.

In the meantime I'd been checking the want ads in *Editor & Publisher*, which had a plentiful supply of openings for journalists in those days, and even a few for artists and cartoonists. I had already missed out on an opening at the *Providence Journal-Bulletin* in Rhode Island. But the next *E&P* ad I answered was in much-closer Albuquerque. At least moving expenses would be lower! I updated my résumé and sent some sample drawings off to the *Albuquerque Journal*, hoping for the best.

3. 7th and Silver

In the late fall of 1976 I settled into my new job as the staff editorial cartoonist for New Mexico's largest daily newspaper, the morning *Albuquerque Journal*. Our offices were in a three-story brick building in Albuquerque's rather small downtown area at the corner of 7th St. and Silver Ave. My drawing board was squeezed into the passageway between the cubicles for the editorial page staff and the cloakroom, up on the third floor, which also housed the Associated Press and UPI. The newsroom proper was on the second floor, along with the separate offices of our sister paper and competition, the afternoon *Albuquerque Tribune*, an affiliate of the Scripps-Howard chain of newspapers based in Cincinnati. During the Depression, the two papers had entered into the nation's first JOA, or Joint Operating Agreement, in which they shared advertising, circulation, and production facilities while the editorial and reporting operations remained separate. Though we competed against each other, the staffs were friendly, often lunching together in the canteen and socializing at the local press club. At the time, the morning *Journal*'s circulation was well over one hundred thousand while the afternoon *Tribune*'s was about forty thousand. The *Tribune* had its own editorial cartoonist, Jerry Bittle, an excellent artist who left a couple of years later and created the comic strip *Geech*. He was succeeded by Mark Taylor until the late 1980s.

My daily routine usually began with the editorial-page staff enjoying morning coffee around 10:00 a.m. at a nearby coffee shop or restaurant, followed by the editorial board meeting in Editor Jerry Crawford's office. I'd spend the rest of the morning reading newspapers and scribbling down thoughts for possible cartoons, grab a brown-bag lunch downstairs in the canteen or go out to a nearby café, and then buckle down to do the next day's cartoon. I needed to start the finished drawing, which would take a couple of hours, by four o'clock or so if I was to meet the deadline for the first edition. Then I'd show it to the editorial-page editor, Eric McCrossen, and run it downstairs to the composing room to be photographed. A print, called a velox, would be made and pasted up on the page.

Early on I would finish my cartoon first before getting it okayed by my editor. This was running the risk of it not being approved for publication, but that hadn't been a problem yet. However, one week in 1977, when the *Journal* was running stories every day about the local science fair, there came a story about the Army testifying at a US Senate hearing that it was no longer conducting open-air testing of biological warfare agents at Dugway Proving Grounds in Utah, which had been the site of a mysterious killing in 1968 of several thousand sheep on a nearby ranch. For some reason I thought it would be humorous to connect the two by having the Army exhibiting its nerve-gas experiment at the science fair. When I showed the finished cartoon to Eric, he said he thought he'd better run it by the editors in the newsroom downstairs. He returned shortly and reported that the consensus was that it shouldn't run. So that's how I learned what I had somehow missed, that the *Journal* was a major

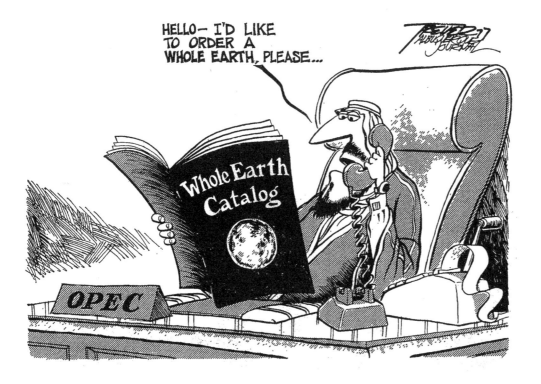

sponsor of the science fair. It was my first killed cartoon. After that I started showing Eric rough sketches before I began inking a final cartoon. Here are a couple of cartoons that did run in my first year at the *Journal*, the first one spoofing the OPEC cartel's control of the world oil market, keeping oil prices high . . .

. . . and this one about Jimmy Carter's controversial plan to hand over control of the Panama Canal Zone to Panama:

Having admired Pat Oliphant's work in the *Denver Post* for eight years since moving west, I was determined to follow his example and produce five editorial cartoons a week, Tuesday through Friday and Sunday. At the same time I had additional assignments for illustrations, spot cartoons, maps, and other graphics to accompany various articles for other departments, so I occasionally had to miss a day's editorial cartoon to handle these other tasks. While they made my workday more hectic, I enjoyed these opportunities to try different styles in other parts of the paper. Usually it was the features department, but sometimes the sports department would tap me for an assignment, such as this drawing for a story previewing the 1977 Indianapolis 500, which featured Al and Bobby Unser, Albuquerque's favorite sons in auto racing.

Nevertheless, I confess I felt some relief when after a couple of years

the *Journal* hired Russ Ball and then Greg Tucker, excellent artists both, to take over the bulk of the illustration duties.

It was one of these additional tasks that brought me my first critical letter-to-the-editor. I think it was my second week at the *Journal* when

I misspelled "Santa Fe" on a locator map for a news article, somehow lettering it "Sante Fe." That got by the editors, too, and we were quickly informed of it by an alert subscriber. There would be many more negative letters, of course, but mostly about my political views or lack of taste, not my spelling, which normally I'm quite attentive to, since fixing mistakes in India ink can be a pain.

Apparently in those first years I had a tendency to resort to clown and circus imagery when cartooning some of the local officials. The county government was a source of much controversy at the time, and I enjoyed caricaturing what I called the "Barnum & Bernalillo County Commission." The school board and various other local and state entities also received this treatment, until it was pointed out to me one day that I was relying too much on this slapstick approach. Point well taken. One thing you don't want in this business is to become too predictable.

I always tried to keep in mind that my main value to the *Journal* was as a local commentator. However, because of my interest in national politics and economic issues, I was doing a fair amount of cartooning on national topics from the start, and I began occasionally sending prints to national magazines that were using editorial cartoons. Early in the Carter administration, six months after I began at the *Journal*, one of my cartoons on Jimmy Carter's proposed fifty-dollar tax rebate, intended to help stimulate the economy, appeared in *Time* magazine.

Coincidentally, *Time*'s royalty check was for fifty dollars. And in appreciation, Parker Brothers sent us a deluxe edition of Monopoly.

Reprints in *U.S. News & World Report*, *National Review*, and *Reason* soon followed, and the next year *Newsweek* used this cartoon on China's opening up to American business, in this case Coca-Cola:

Here are a couple of other typical cartoons from 1978. The first was done after Carter's persistent diplomatic efforts at Camp David finally resulted in Menachem Begin and Anwar Sadat signing the Camp David Accords, leading to the Egypt-Israel Peace Treaty of 1979 and the return of the Sinai Peninsula to Egypt.

Another important event that

year was the selection of the first non-Italian pope in four centuries, John Paul II from Poland, who had survived both Nazi and Soviet occupation and then inspired his nation's Solidarity movement, leading to the eventual end of communism in

Europe. I used a classic cartoon image to commemorate the event:

News Item: The new pope is reported to be an avid skier.

"Trivial Pursuit" may have come out in 1979, but the year had some momentous events, including the Three-Mile Island nuclear plant accident, the Sandinistas take-over in Nicaragua, the Soviet invasion of Afghanistan, and the Iranian Revolution and hostage crisis. Soaring oil prices led to long gas lines and high gas prices, featured in this cartoon . . .

. . . while inflation, interest rates, and gold prices headed to record levels and the dollar weakened.

While my cartoons were getting occasional national exposure in various magazines, my goal was to eventually become syndicated to other newspapers around the country. I was

"WOW! LOOK AT THOSE CRAZY FOOLS GO ZOOMING UP!"

quite happy with my situation at the *Journal* and the lively politics of New Mexico, but it was a relatively small market. One of the paradoxes in political cartooning (indeed, in most of journalism) is the fact that your cartoons have the most influence at the local level, but the greatest influence on your career is from your national cartoons. We are frequently urged to do more cartoons on city and state issues, but that comes at the expense of national recognition. While there are state and regional contests, the prestigious national awards are almost always for cartoons on national and international issues, the simple reason being, I suppose, that the judges would likely be unfamiliar with the issue upon which an otherwise trenchant local cartoon is based.

In hopes of achieving wider circulation, I began entering several of the national journalism contests, thinking that a major award might spark the interest of one of the leading newspaper syndicates. My break came in early 1980, when I was awarded the "Distinguished Service Award" for 1979 editorial cartoons by the Society of Professional Journalists, also known as Sigma Delta Chi (SDX). This entailed travelling to their regional convention in Seattle that year and, at a fancy black-tie banquet, receiving a bronze medallion and a very hefty plaque. The award was for my entry of six cartoons, including the two shown here on the Three-Mile Island nuclear plant accident and the Cambodian genocide:

I also received a very encouraging letter from the chairman of the Pulitzer Prize jury for the editorial cartoon award, saying I'd just missed being a finalist. Although other honors occasionally came my way in the coming years, this would be the closest I would come to that particular award. The SDX prize led to an invite to join the local Sigma Delta Chi chapter, composed of local media and public-relations folks. I served as president of the chapter one year, during which I managed to convince "Bloom County" creator Berke Breathed (who was living in Albuquerque at the time) and mystery-writer Tony Hillerman to address the group.

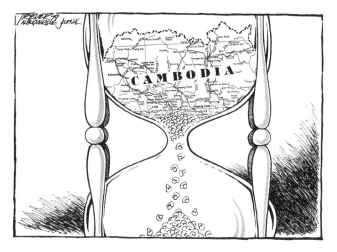

I was already syndicated to many college newspapers through the College Press Service, based in Denver, and I felt that now was the time to test the waters for national syndication. Energized by the SDX honor, I began sending portfolios to all of the major national syndicates, including King Features, United Features Syndicate, and Field Newspaper Syndicate. No offers for individual syndication were immediately forthcoming, but two syndicates expressed interest for including me in their editorial cartoon "packages." Copley News Service, based in southern California, would distribute my work as part of their various services.

At the same time Field Enterprises, owned by the Chicago Sun-Times, offered to include me in a just-launched group syndication of six cartoonists. The editorial cartoon "package" was a new marketing idea that was intended to appeal to a lot of the small and mid-sized dailies that might have difficulty paying for two or three individually syndicated political cartoonists. For the price of one Oliphant or MacNelly or Herblock feature, they could get a packet of five cartoons a day, five days a week, from several cartoonists from different parts of the country and with different political outlooks.

In June of 1980, while Copley had started to distribute my work (a looser affiliation without a contract), I decided to sign with the Field syndicate and become part of their package. The *Journal* was very supportive, even providing one of the lawyers from the company's legal firm to help negotiate the syndicate contract. The package was called "The Best and the Wittiest," which we cartoonists thought was a bit of embarrassing marketing hype, but it sold well, with over three hundred clients, both big and small papers. Besides myself, the original roster of editorial cartoonists included Mike Keefe of the *Denver Post*, the *San Diego Union*'s Lee Judge (who soon moved to the *Kansas City Star*), Gary Brookins of the *Richmond Times-Dispatch*, Bob Gorrell of the *Charlotte News* (later of the *Richmond News-Leader*), Bill Deore of the *Dallas Morning News*, and Brian Bassett of the *Seattle Times*. When Rupert Murdoch acquired the *Sun-Times* and Field Enterprises in 1983, the syndicate was renamed News America Syndicate, and then, three years later, when it was sold to the Hearst Corporation, it became the North America Syndicate, a division of their King Features Syndicate.

Over the years the lineup of contributors to the package went through many changes as new cartoonists were added, others dropped out, and some went on to individual syndication, but the feature has retained its original title. Typically the syndicate wouldn't use every cartoon I sent, but they did send out a large majority of them. Initially the revenue was split 50-50 between the syndicate and the six contributors. Later King turned it into a piece-work operation, with each of us getting paid a flat fee for each cartoon they included in the package. It certainly was no way to get rich, but we did appreciate the wide circulation of the feature, and the monthly checks, however small, were a welcome bonus. The advantage of the package concept for me was its flexibility. Instead of being obligated to provide the syndicate with three to five cartoons on national topics each and every week, I could devote more attention to local subjects when needed, such as when the Legislature was in session, and know my package partners would be taking up any slack. We were rarely aware of where our cartoons were appearing, so it was always a treat whenever a friend or colleague came back from a vacation trip with one of my cartoons they'd seen in some distant town's paper.

In 1977 Jeff MacNelly capitalized on his wide editorial cartoon syndication by creating a comic strip, *Shoe*, featuring a cast of birds producing the *Treetops Tattler-Tribune*, based on some of his colleagues and friends. It was an immediate success, and suddenly the newspaper syndicates began to look to editorial cartoonists as a possible source for new comic strips. I presume this was because they had a proven track record, demonstrating the ability to produce cartoons week after week, year after year, and thus would be a safer bet than a promising but unproven talent. This had been the case within the comic-strip business for years, of course, as established artists such as Al Capp (*Li'l Abner*, *Abbie & Slats*, *Long Sam*), Mort Walker (*Beetle Bailey*, *Hi & Lois*, *Boner's Ark*), and Johnny Hart (*B.C.*, *Wizard of Id*) were regular comic-strip factories, with numerous assistants. The success of *Shoe* inspired the syndicates to seek out willing political cartoonists, and soon a number of them were doubling up and producing strips of their own: Doug Marlette began *Kudzu*, Mike Peters created *Mother Goose & Grimm*, Bill Schorr launched *The Grizzwells*, Brian Bassett drew *Adam* and later *Red and Rover*, and Scott Stantis started *The Buckets* as well as *Prickly City*, to name a few. Even Pat Oliphant got into the act for a while with a color Sunday strip called *Sunday Punk*.

At one point I was also approached by a couple of syndicates to do a comic feature. I asked, "What kind?" hoping they had something specific in mind, but they said, "Up to you." Given the amount of effort I devoted to my daily editorial cartoon, I doubted adding a 365-days-a-year comic strip would be a good idea. By that time I had realized that whatever talent I had was in reacting to events, not in creating a whole new comic world from scratch. But I thought maybe I could do a simple edit page "filler" feature, like *Small Society*, using my leftover ideas that never made it into a full-fledged cartoons. So I worked up a few samples of something I called *Spotshots* and sent it to a couple of syndicates. Fortunately for my health and sanity they decided not to go ahead with it.

It has frequently been noted that editorial cartooning is a lonely profession. Unlike the other journalists in the formerly well-populated newsroom, you are the sole practitioner at your newspaper—often even in your city or your state. This was particularly true in the West, where you could be separated from your nearest colleague by hundreds of miles. Of course there was always the telephone, and some cartoonists of my acquaintance conferred regularly by phone. But often the only opportunity for face-to-face conversations, talking shop, socializing, kibitzing, and networking was at the annual convention of our professional society, the Association of American Editorial Cartoonists (AAEC), which I had joined in 1973. Any isolation I felt in Albuquerque was mitigated somewhat by the fact that, at least early on, our sister paper, the *Tribune*, had a cartoonist with whom to compare notes. In the 1980s, the small cartoonist fraternity in Albuquerque would gather for an annual picnic, which was often hosted by Nate Butler, who freelanced for Archie Comics, assisted on the *Snuffy Smith* strip, and later founded a Christian comics mission. Also in attendance would be the illustrators from both papers and the occasional caricaturist or computer animator in town.

The AAEC had several hundred members in those days, including some from Canada and Mexico. The annual conventions would be held, usually in the summer, in various cities around the country, where a local newspaper could help sponsor the three- to five-day event. Besides the opportunity to meet fellow cartoonists and catch up on the latest news, tools, and trends in our field, there would be seminars, panel discussions, sightseeing excursions, banquets, and plenty of time, of course, to party. The conventions afforded some fond memories, particularly the 1979 convention in relatively close Phoenix, which was my first chance to visit with many of the artists I knew only from their cartoons. This was the beginning of several friendships. Our whole family attended the Nashville convention in 1981, where I could indulge my love of bluegrass music, which was followed by a visit to my brother and his family in Pensacola, Florida. In 1982, at the San Francisco convention, an excursion to Napa Valley and a luncheon at the Robert Mondavi winery helped spark my continuing interest in wine. The 1984 convention in Oklahoma City was a chance to meet Bill Mauldin and see an exhibit of his *Willie and Joe* cartoons at the headquarters of his old Army unit. *Seattle Times* cartoonist Brian Bassett and I took in a Chicago Cubs game at Wrigley Field during the 1988 convention in nearby Milwaukee. At the 1993 Austin convention, host cartoonist and fellow railroad buff Ben Sargent invited me to ride in the locomotive cab on a steam-train excursion.

The conventions usually featured a speech by a notable political figure, activist, or journalist. Over the years we heard from politicians such as Barry Goldwater, Mario Cuomo, Walter Mondale, governors Jerry Brown and Dick Lamm, House Speaker Tom Foley, and senators Alan Cranston and Paul Wellstone, who would address some of the issues we dealt with in our work. Some members questioned whether this was useful, feeling they were just getting standard political boilerplate, while others thought it was helpful to have some prominent names on the schedule to convince their editors to send them to the convention. Then there were political activists like Tom Hayden, Charlton Heston (when he was the NRA president), and Ben Cohen (of Ben & Jerry's Ice Cream), who addressed issues they thought we *should* be dealing with. Other notables I can recall were author Gore Vidal, country singer Tom T. Hall, *New Yorker* cartoonist George Booth, radio personality Garrison Keillor, and journalist Molly Ivins. Pat Oliphant was the banquet speaker at the 1987 Washington, DC, convention, where he poured gasoline on the smoldering controversy over the Pulitzer Board's awarding of that year's editorial cartooning prize to a comic strip, *Bloom County*, by Berke Breathed, who subsequently offered his rejoinder at the following year's banquet. Most of the cartoonists would doodle away on these occasions to see who could do the best caricature of the speaker, who would often be presented with some of the resulting sketches.

Like any large group, the AAEC personalities ran the gamut from Life of the Party to Quiet Introvert. Some seemed to feel it important to live up to the image of cartoonists as Class Clowns and "Wild and Crazy Guys." Others were just interested in renewing friendships and catching up on the latest scuttlebutt. There was a certain amount of cliquishness, of course, with the older, more established cartoonists hanging out together, while younger cartoonists flocked around the latest Pulitzer winner or Syndicate Star. What I found interesting, though, was the lack of political discussion or debate among the cartoonists themselves. Perhaps it was because we all were pretty aware of where our colleagues were on the political spectrum and avoided controversy in a desire to maintain a convivial atmosphere. We would be quite liberal with our compliments about the quality of each other's work, even if we disagreed with its political viewpoint. Often talk turned to our outside interests and hobbies instead. *Detroit News* cartoonist Larry Wright and I were both interested in model trains, and one year we found a nearby toy-train show to attend. Mike Keefe had run marathons, and several of the younger cartoonists at the Phoenix convention joined him for a morning run, which they probably later regretted. A few, such as Steve Kelley from the *San Diego Union-Tribune*, who has appeared on *The Tonight Show*, even do stand-up comedy in their spare time. Several had some music talent and would bring musical instruments—a guitar, a banjo, a harmonica—and gather around the hotel piano for jam sessions after hours. A semi-organized group called themselves the "Toon Tones" and would play after the banquet while others, assisted by ample quantities of beer, would try to sing along.

I enjoyed the AAEC confabs for many years, even serving as an officer for several years in the late 1980s, but then my attendance began to wane as I remarried, our kids got involved in youth sports and other activities, and we embarked on overseas travel. As a result, I'm afraid, I began to lose touch with all but a few of my fellow cartoonists.

4. *Journal Center*

*A*ll this time the *Journal* was growing in circulation and staff and outgrowing our downtown Albuquerque quarters. In the early 1980s we began moving everything to a spacious campus in our own business park, the Journal Center, in the North I-25 corridor. By 1985 I had my own office, complete with a sink and built-in cabinets and bookshelves, plus ample space for several file cabinets—which quickly became overstuffed, of course.

The *Journal*'s new presses and increased circulation also enabled the creation of extra editions. We had had two editions all along: the "State," the early press run delivered to the outlying areas of New Mexico; and the "Final," the second run intended for the Albuquerque metropolitan area. Several regional editions were now created by remaking the local news section, first the "Journal North" for Santa Fe and its environs, then the "Metro Plus" edition for the growing west side of Albuquerque and Rio Rancho, followed by a "Journal South" edition. Later "Metro Plus" was divided into separate "West Side" and "Rio Rancho" editions. Even my printed cartoon grew in size when, after an edit-page redesign in 1987, it was enlarged from three columns to four columns wide. I remember this well because the first several cartoons I drew in the new format were on the big Wall Street crash that fall. This prominent display lasted for over a decade until the *Journal* began shrinking in width, a reaction to the rising price of newsprint.

It wasn't long before the "Metro Plus" edition started its own editorial page once a week and I was asked to create a cartoon for it. Suddenly I found my workload increasing 20 percent to six cartoons a week, but I was able to juggle my routine so that one day a week I was able to do the Metro Plus cartoon in the morning and my regular cartoon in the afternoon. This schedule lasted for about fifteen years until falling circulation and advertising occasioned by the 2000 recession and the encroaching internet led to cutbacks in the extra editions.

In the late '80s I was approached by the Albuquerque Public Schools about taking part in their student mentorship program. I agreed to do it with the stipulation that the student was serious about cartooning and was contributing cartoons or illustrations to a school publication. The mentorships would last a semester, and I would meet once a week with the student at my office. We would discuss various cartooning topics, and I'd make an assignment that would be critiqued the following week. The assignments were very loosely based on my old Famous Artists School cartoon course. I conducted a half-dozen or more of these mentorships with students of varying degrees of talent, but I don't believe any of them eventually pursued cartooning as a career—lucky for them, I suppose, given the shrunken state of the field these days.

One thing newspaper cartoonists and artists discover early on is that they are the go-to person when it comes to presentations at farewell or retirement parties for one of the staff. When called upon I would contribute a cartoon or caricature featuring the honoree, but the illustrators probably handled the lion's share of these events, and at times the design desk might work up a mock newspaper page for the retiree. The staff would crowd into the conference room to hear praises, funny stories, and farewell wishes for the departing colleague, who would say how great it had been working with us and how much we'd be missed. Then the presentations would be made, the cake cut, the coffee served, and we'd return to our desks on a brief sugar high.

In addition to these in-house requests, I would get occasional calls for outside freelance projects. These would usually be for a caricature of some poor soul marking a special milestone such as a birthday or retirement. Since I didn't consider caricature my strong suit and I had enough trouble doing politicians at work, I very often referred these requests to one of the local caricaturists in town. It helps to learn to say "no" at times, no matter how much they say they love your work. I did have a firm policy of not doing cartoons, or even allowing reprints, for political candidates, in the interests of maintaining my editorial independence.

But one caricature project that I did say "yes" to turned out to be quite an ambitious effort. The Greater Albuquerque Chamber of Commerce each spring gave out appreciation awards to state legislators who had helped with their legislative goals for that session, and one year they approached me to do a series of caricatures that would be framed and given to the recipients, instead of the usual plaques. I accepted the commission, not only because the remuneration made it worth my while, but because it was an interesting challenge: while nearly all of my editorial cartoons were critical and negative in nature, here was an opportunity to create cartoons that were actually positive instead (and hopefully clever and/or amusing).

The project would take up several weekends each spring to do the twenty or so caricatures, but the recipients were good sports about the results, and it was an interesting change of approach from my usual work.

Another frequent source of requests is from politicians or regular readers asking to buy original drawings or prints of a cartoon that had appeared in the paper. The original could just be slipped into a large envelope for pick-up or mailing. Prints would require a visit to a copy shop to get a good quality image on heavy stock, then matting it and inserting it into a protective sleeve. I charged a modest fee for the original drawings and a fraction of that for the prints. Some I would donate for charitable

Two 2006 legislator awards for facilitating development of Spaceport America.

purposes. I would sell or donate a dozen or two originals a year, but most of them accumulated in boxes in my cabinets at work or in closets at home. Soon after I retired I arranged to donate these to the special collections departments of the libraries at Syracuse University, which received my national-subject originals, and the University of New Mexico, which received the cartoons on New Mexico topics. No doubt my wife, Karen, was greatly relieved.

In 1994 I was invited by Mary Ann Weems to be part of her eclectic art gallery, beginning with a one-man show of some of my cartoon originals. Mary Ann was an energetic, enthusiastic entrepreneur, a force of nature really, and by the following year she had talked me into having a booth at her annual Weems Artfest at the State Fairgrounds. This involved considerable time and investment in framing and matting the cartoons and prints, and then much effort, greatly aided by my wife, in decorating and setting up the booth, but it was always an enjoyable weekend and a great opportunity to meet readers, get feedback and suggestions, and even sell a few pieces. In 2009, however, I somehow managed to double-book Artfest weekend and commit to a speaking engagement at a college reunion affair in Las Vegas. Luckily my son David was able to man the booth, so after we opened the show, Karen and I flew to Vegas and returned on Sunday in time to be there for the last few hours. I continued exhibiting until I retired, and for a couple more years after that, culminating in 2013 when Mary Ann presented me the Artfest's "Art Icon" award. The gallery has continued to carry a few originals, prints, and books.

One of my best sellers at the Weems Artfest was the books. In the late '80s I began discussing with the editors the possibility of doing a cartoon collection, and by 1992 *The Trever Gallery: A Public Hanging* had been published by the *Journal* and printed by its job-printing affiliate, Starline Printing. With the encouragement of publisher Tom Lang and editor Jerry Crawford, the help of my edit-page colleagues Steve Mills and Bill Hume, who wrote the introduction, and Bill Lang and his staff at Starline, we were able to put together a volume that contained over 280 of my national and international cartoons covering the Reagan and George H. W. Bush years. Starline had a high-quality six-color press, which, while not crucial to this book's contents, was important to the cover, which required me to leave the security of my black-and-white world and create a full-color drawing. The *Journal* advertised the book extensively, and I did the obligatory signings at local independent book-stores and plugged it at my occasional speaking gigs. Sales were decent, but I don't suppose it was a threat to make the best-seller lists. Political cartoon books are not like regular cartoon books because they're . . . well . . . *political*, and about half your potential customer base may not be very receptive. Nevertheless it sold well at the Artfests and seemed to be a popular choice for holiday gifting.

Seven years later it was time to try again, and we published a second collection of my cartoons, *The Trever GallerY2K: Drawing Fire*, which covered national and international issues during the Clinton presidency. The "GallerY2K" in the title was a clumsy effort to capitalize on the growing concern in 1999 over the "Millennium Bug" and what would happen to computers when the year 2000 arrived, which turned out to be not much and quickly dated the book. On the plus side, New Mexi-co's senior senator Pete Domenici generously contributed a very compli-mentary foreword, and this volume represented another of my attempts at a color cover. It managed to rack up some decent sales, often person-ally dedicated and signed by me at various venues, including the Artfest.

Up to this point these collected works featured only examples of my syndicated cartoons. I was neglecting an obvious mother lode of material, as was occasionally pointed out by friends and acquaintances: namely New Mexico, whose politics had occupied half of my output. Finally, after much urging and some false starts, a third book comprised of over 350 state and local cartoons appeared in 2007. It was titled *Mañana Republic* and sported an improved color cover, featuring a hot-air balloon with a Roundhouse basket occupied by a gaggle of New Mexico politicos. By this time I'd wised up and simply created a color key for my black-and-white cover drawing and handed it over to the computer wizards at Starline to fill in the colors. Independent bookstores were starting to dis-appear, but I did a few signings, and the *Journal* hosted a special event for the book. I was kept very busy signing books at the 2007 Artfest, and *Mañana Republic* continued to sell well through the Great Recession, when the sales of originals and prints dried up.

As the first decade of the twenty-first century drew to a close, I was giving serious thought to retirement from my daily grind. With the dot-com crash, the 9/11 attacks, the Iraq War, the onset of the Great Reces-sion, and the Obamacare battle, as well as the end of the Gary Johnson administration and the eight hyperactive years of Bill Richardson in Santa Fe, there was no lack of cartoon opportunities to keep me engaged. But the kids were grown and gone (most of the time), Karen was retired from Montessori teaching, and I found myself reading articles on Social Security and financial planning a lot. In addition, recession and the challenges posed by the internet were taking their toll on the *Journal*, as circulation declined and the staff shrunk through attrition and layoffs. While I felt secure in my job, unlike so many of my colleagues at other papers, I increasingly felt the desire to slow down. One day in 2010, I sat down with Editor Kent Walz in his big corner office and announced my intention to retire. I would be happy to step aside completely to allow the *Journal* to hire a full-time replacement if they wished, although given the state of the business, I thought it unlikely. (Nevertheless, when I mentioned my plans to friends at my last AAEC convention in Portland, Oregon, that summer, the *Journal* received a flurry of applications). Or I could stay on part-time, I suggested, and do a cartoon once a week for the Sunday paper. The *Journal* seemed happy with that, so we worked out a brief agreement for me to become a "consultant." I would come into the office on Fridays, try to catch up on the newsroom gossip, and crank out a local cartoon. Since I dressed casual the rest of the week, it would be formal Friday for me. I looked forward to the six-day weekend, but I didn't look forward to cleaning out my office and its accumulations of over three decades. That would probably take another decade, I feared. The process has started several times, but here we are, a decade later and still accumulating.

5. Twenty-First Century Limited

It was my intent when I retired to deal with just state and local topics in my Sunday cartoons—otherwise the *Journal* wouldn't have
any local cartoon commentary at all, since the syndicated offerings
we used the rest of the week were necessarily national in scope. Thus,
after contributing to the "Best and Wittiest" package for thirty years,
I reluctantly informed King Features that I was retiring from full-time
cartooning and also my syndication at the end of 2010. Though they
said they'd be willing to accept less-frequent cartoons, I knew that
would be only one or two (and usually none) per year, since New Mexico issues are rarely on the national radar screen (immigration might be
an exception). However, since
my national cartoons had last
been collected in a book over
twenty years ago, what follows
is a sampling of my syndicated
national cartoons through 2010,
plus a few extras.

The start of the new Millennium was anticipated with a healthy dose of dread, as worries, warnings, and fears grew that the world's computers would be flummoxed by the so-called Millennium Bug, because they would recognize the "00" in dates as "1900" instead of "2000." This could create computer shutdowns and massive confusion. Despite much time and money being spent in trying to avert the problem, anxiety over the "Y2K Bug" remained widespread. However, when January 1, 2000, finally arrived, there were few problems.

A bigger glitch would come with the 2000 presidential election later in the year. The political season started off normally enough, with Vice President Al Gore easily sewing up his party's nomination by Super Tuesday in March, as did Texas Governor George W. Bush after a battle with Sen. John McCain of Arizona. New Mexico, holding its primary in June, as usual had no impact on the nominations.

Bush proposed strengthening the Social Security system by allowing accounts to be invested in the stock market. Gore promised to protect Social Security in a "lockbox."

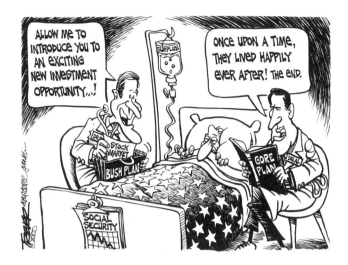

Bush named his father's former VP Dick Cheney to head up a search committee to select a running mate, which turned out to be: Dick Cheney!

The election came down to the wire and was too close to call on election night. The result hinged on the vote in Florida, which Bush led by a tiny margin, requiring a recount.

Political operatives and lawyers from both parties hastened to Florida to observe and contest the various county recounts. The battle lasted past Thanksgiving.

In counties using punch-card ballots, some of the votes for president were incompletely punched out, leading to "hanging chads," "pregnant chads," or "dimpled chads."

Depending on which incompletely punched ballots were allowed, either Gore or Bush would gain or lose votes.

With the deadline for the states to certify their votes to the Electoral College looming, the Bush lawyers appealed the Florida Supreme Court decision to continue recounts of contested ballots to the Supreme Court . . .

. . . .which ruled 5–4 that Bush's official 537-vote margin should stand, giving George Bush all of Florida's electoral votes and a 271–266 margin in the Electoral College, and making it one of the closest in history. It was the fourth US presidential election in which the winner lost the popular vote.

Because of the election controversy and his narrow victory, Bush entered the White House with little political momentum and with the economy beginning a mild recession.

He managed to push through a tax cut bill as well as the No Child Left Behind Act, the latest attempt at education reform.

On September 11, terrorists flew hijacked planes into New York's World Trade Center and the Pentagon and killed nearly three thousand people, more than at Pearl Harbor, changing the world and Bush's presidency forever.

Similar cartoons, featuring a grieving Statue of Liberty, appeared across the country, as the attack united the nation, with a few exceptions . . .

The economic shocks from the attack included a sharp drop on global stock markets and a worsening US recession, prompting appeals for consumers to keep buying.

Osama Bin Laden and Al Qaeda were quickly found to be responsible for the attacks, and Bush declared a War on Terror to bring them to justice. In October, American and British forces launched airstrikes and invaded Afghanistan, no stranger to foreign invaders, to oust the Taliban regime, which harbored Bin Laden, beginning America's longest war.

Clues to an impending attack had existed prior to 9/11, but the plot went undetected because a legal "wall" had developed between intelligence and law-enforcement functions that prevented information sharing.

The USA PATRIOT Act was quickly passed to detect and prevent future attacks, but the enhanced law-enforcement and surveillance powers raised civil-liberties concerns.

A new cabinet department, the Department of Homeland Security, was created to consolidate numerous functions from other departments, including the Coast Guard, border security, immigration, customs, anti-terrorism, and disaster management, but it was feared such a big bureaucracy would be unwieldy and ineffective.

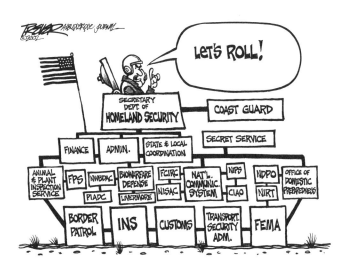

The first anniversary of 9/11 was the occasion for multiple tributes, observances, and events.

On the domestic front, Bush announced tariffs on certain types on foreign steel to help the struggling American steel producers.

Congress passed a huge farm bill, criticized as "agribusiness welfare," for large corporate farmers, with billions in subsidies for crops in key swing states in the midterm elections.

Proposals to further increase automobile fuel standards raised concerns that vehicle downsizing and weight reduction would lead to more traffic fatalities.

Amtrak continued to limp along, heavily subsidized and lightly utilized, except for the new "high-speed" Acela in the populous Northeast Corridor, which was mostly slowed by poor trackage.

The Supreme Court upheld a school-choice plan in Cleveland, which used public funds for tuition vouchers to attend private schools, including religious ones.

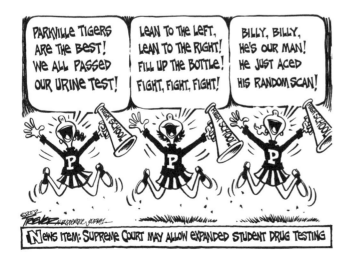

In another case, the court considered, and later upheld, the use of random drug testing of public high school students engaged in extracurricular activities.

There were increasing reports of outbreaks of adult violence at youth sports contests.

Claims of child sex abuse by Catholic priests in the Boston Archdiocese became a widening scandal, echoing the pedophile priest scandal in New Mexico ten years before.

In the Middle East, despite earlier assurances that he would be a "partner for peace," Yasser Arafat rejected the 2000 Clinton-Ehud Barak peace plan at Camp David and the Palestinians began a second "intifada" against Israeli control of the West Bank, capped by a wave a suicide bombings . . .

. . . and prompting Israel's new prime minister, Ariel Sharon, to send the Israeli army on a destructive operation to reoccupy the West Bank and corner Arafat in his Ramallah headquarters. Bush demanded that Sharon pull back his forces.

A "Roadmap for Peace" to resolve the conflict, crafted by the United States, the United Nations, the European Union, and Russia, was released. Newly appointed Palestinian Prime Minister Mahmoud Abbas accepted the plan, but Sharon objected to a freeze of Israeli settlements, and continued terrorist bombings would eventually scuttle the plan.

Meanwhile, North Korea was believed to be in violation of the 1994 Agreed Framework to freeze its nuclear weapons program and was seeking additional US concessions.

In the aftermath of 9/11, the Bush administration began building support for removing Saddam Hussein from power in Iraq, which it called a member of the "Axis of Evil" (Iran, Iraq, and North Korea), claiming that his brutal regime had links to Al Qaeda, was continuing to develop weapons of mass destruction, and was committing human-rights abuses.

The UN Security Council, unconvinced that Iraq was a threat and hoping to stave off an American invasion, drafted a resolution giving Iraq a "final opportunity" to comply with UN inspections and disarm.

The diplomatic maneuvering continued as the United States argued that Saddam had not given a full accounting of Iraq's weapons and was manipulating the process to buy time, but the United Nations resisted a new resolution authorizing force and supported further inspections.

While Congress also supported a diplomatic solution, it had voted earlier to authorize force against the Saddam regime if diplomacy failed. On March 17 Bush declared that diplomacy had failed, and he issued an ultimatum for Saddam to leave Iraq in forty-eight hours, immediately rejected by Saddam. Two days later, the United States, the United Kingdom, and a small "coalition of the willing" began the invasion. I was reminded of Julius Caesar when he crossed a certain river on his way to Rome.

The allied forces launched a "shock and awe" campaign of airstrikes on Baghdad. Saddam remained defiant.

US troops made rapid progress and seized Baghdad in three weeks, but every time they paused in the advance, the news media, like "generals fighting the last war," would fret about potential setbacks.

Bush declared the end of "major combat operations" as Iraqis celebrated the downfall of Saddam. The war had not become a quagmire, but the postwar would be a different story, as the country soon become embroiled in outbreaks of looting, bombings, and attacks from insurgent Iraqi fighters.

Despite years of official warnings regarding Saddam's WMDs, Bush's claims were met with increasing skepticism . . .

. . . which was borne out when US inspector David Kay reported a few remnants but no stockpiles . . .

. . . necessitating another investigation . . .

. . . which concluded that the intelligence community had made faulty assessments.

In December of 2003, outside Saddam's hometown of Tikrit, US troops discovered the bedraggled dictator hiding in a hole . . .

... and sent him to prison to await trial by his countrymen.

The federal government redesigned the currency, while war costs, tax cuts, and new spending initiatives quickly turned a modest budget surplus into a big deficit . . .

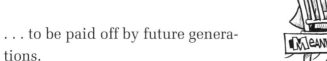

... to be paid off by future generations.

Pope John Paul II died after helping to bring about historic change, putting to rest an old joke.

In health news, the prevalence of obesity in the US population was becoming a leading cause of death.

A decline in the number of vaccine producers led to a serious shortage during the 2004 flu season.

In the sports world, a vote-fixing scandal for the gold medal in the pairs skating competition at the 2002 Salt Lake City Winter Olympics increased demands for changes to the subjective judging system . . .

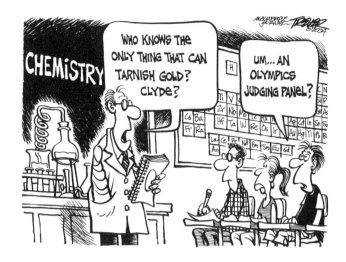

. . . while Major League Baseball was rocked by ongoing revelations of steroid use, which would lead to Congressional hearings.

In the 2004 presidential election, the issue of military experience, ignored in the Clinton years, suddenly became relevant again as the Democratic nomination was locked up by Vietnam veteran and Purple Heart recipient, Massachusetts senator John Kerry . . .

. . . whose campaign, however, was quickly bogged down in controversies over his war record and subsequent testimony about war crimes.

Meanwhile Ralph Nader, formerly a Green Party candidate, whom Democrats blamed for Gore's loss in Florida, started petition drives to get on the 2004 ballot as an independent.

While Republicans worried about improper voter registrations, the Democrats contested Nader's petitions in many states.

Weakened by the controversies over his war record, Kerry focused on other issues and gained in the polls during the presidential debates.

Then Bush's military service became an issue when CBS uncovered memos that seemed to indicate he hadn't properly completed his Air National Guard obligation.

But the memos soon proved to be fakes, and CBS anchorman Dan Rather, who initially insisted on their accuracy, later resigned.

By election day, the race was quite close. Early media exit polls predicted a Kerry win, but when Ohio finally went for Bush the next day, Bush was declared the winner.

But the year had not gone well for efforts at reconstruction and democratization in post-Saddam Iraq. A newly established Coalition Provisional Authority abruptly dissolved the Iraqi military and ended many government services, leading to high unemployment, rioting, and the beginning of a militant insurgency against Coalition forces.

To make matters worse, at the infamous Abu Ghraib prison, site of torture and mass executions during the Saddam regime, human-rights abuses against Iraqi detainees by US military and CIA personnel employing "enhanced interrogation techniques" were made public, causing worldwide condemnation.

The Coalition transferred limited powers to an Iraqi caretaker government, which immediately put Saddam Hussein on trial.

In early 2005 elections were held to form a National Assembly, which would draft a new constitution.

Meanwhile, Russia's Vladimir Putin, upset by increasing American influence in the former Soviet republics, tried to sway the contested 2004 Ukrainian presidential election in favor of the pro-Russian candidate.

Bush met with Putin several times in hopes that Russia would democratize, including a working meeting in 2005 when Putin let Bush drive his 1956 Volga, but the former KGB officer had different ideas.

A new strain of avian influenza was reported to be spreading rapidly through eastern Asia, and Kim Jong-Il's North Korea regime announced it had produced nuclear weapons . . .

. . . and, the following year, that it had successfully tested one.

President Bush claimed his reelection victory had earned him "political capital," which he determined to use to reform the underfunded Social Security system. The ambitious but controversial plan, which involved giving younger workers the option of diverting a portion of their Social Security taxes into personal retirement accounts with a higher rate of return, went nowhere against strong opposition from Democrats and an increasingly skeptical public.

Despite anti-Coalition attacks and sectarian violence, Iraqi voters ratified a new constitution, and the difficult job of forming a new government began.

In late August the category-5 hurricane Katrina hit the US Gulf coast, causing catastrophic damage and extensive casualties, particularly in New Orleans, which suffered deadly flooding due to the failure of numerous levees.

The emergency disaster response of federal, state, and local authorities caused widespread condemnation and an outbreak of finger-pointing. Bush came in for his share of criticism, as did the Federal Emergency Management Administration, the governor of Louisiana, the mayor of New Orleans, and later the Army Corps of Engineers for design and construction deficiencies in the levee system.

Special Prosecutor Patrick Fitzgerald, appointed to investigate whether the White House had improperly leaked the covert status of CIA operative Valerie Plame, learned early on the leak came from a State Department official but nevertheless continued the investigation for two more years, eventually indicting Lewis "Scooter" Libby for perjury and obstruction of justice.

Bush's "political capital," drained by Iraq, the failed Social Security effort, Katrina, an exploding budget deficit, and his abortive nomination of White House Counsel Harriet Miers to the Supreme Court, had vanished by the end of 2005.

In its effort to prevent terrorist attacks, the expansion of government law-enforcement and surveillance powers was blamed for eroding civil liberties.

The Transportation Security Administration's airport inspections became increasingly intrusive.

Vice President Dick Cheney accidently shot a companion while hunting in Texas.

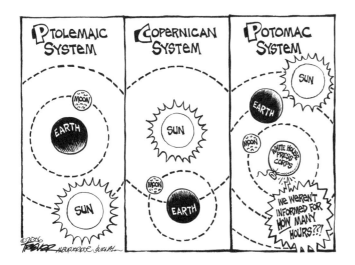

The Washington press corps was highly incensed that the incident wasn't reported until the next day, and by the local Corpus Christi newspaper.

While the international community was suspicious that Iran was diverting material from its nuclear power program to developing nuclear weapons, Iran's president Mahmoud Ahmadinejad drew widespread condemnation for calling the Holocaust a "myth" and a "lie."

After several years of unproductive negotiations over halting Iran's uranium-enrichment program, the United Nations threatened to impose sanctions; Iran offered to resume negotiations.

Hit by declining sales and rising costs, the Ford Motor Co. announced a restructuring plan that would close fourteen plants and shrink its work force by up to thirty thousand jobs.

The official solar system also shrunk when Pluto, discovered in 1930 by New Mexican Clyde Tombaugh, was demoted to a "dwarf planet."

A tough immigration bill featuring stronger border security and classifying illegal immigrants as felons passed the House in late 2005. In reaction, widespread national protests in the spring of 2006 demanded a more comprehensive immigration reform and a "path to citizenship" for undocumented immigrants.

The Senate passed a more lenient bill, supported by President Bush, which enhanced border security but also provided a path for immigrants in the country illegally to obtain legal status, a provision that opponents termed "amnesty" for lawbreakers.

Congress was unable to reconcile the two immigration bills, instead passing a "Secure Fence Act" authorizing construction of seven hundred miles of fencing at the Mexican border.

In Lebanon, Hezbollah forces launched rocket attacks and a cross-border raid into northern Israel, killing several Israeli soldiers and taking two prisoner, demanding Israel release Lebanese prisoners in exchange. Israel responded with airstrikes on Hezbollah and Lebanese targets, a major ground invasion into southern Lebanon, and an air and naval blockade.

In Cuba, an ailing Fidel Castro handed over presidential duties to his brother Raul, commander in chief of the armed forces.

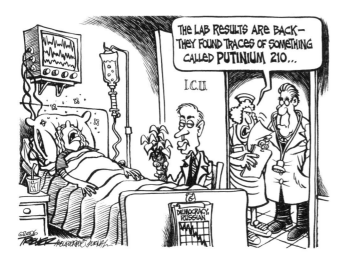

Alexander Litvinenko, a former Russian KGB officer and critic of Vladimir Putin living in Britain, became severely ill and died from radiation poisoning, later determined to be from polonium-210. In a deathbed statement, Litvinenko blamed Putin for his poisoning.

The Supreme Court rejected the sweeping powers claimed by Bush in the detention and trial of war-on-terror detainees at Guantanamo Bay, ruling that the president needed to abide by the Geneva Convention and American law in military tribunals.

Alarmed by the increasing violence, sectarian strife, and possible civil war in Iraq and concerned that the Bush policies were failing, Congress appointed the Iraq Study Group, a bipartisan ten-member panel, to assess the situation and propose a new course of action.

In the 2006 midterm elections, Bush's growing unpopularity due to the Iraq War, the Katrina response, and Social Security proposals, as well as several corruption scandals involving Republican congressmen, had the GOP majorities in jeopardy . . .

. . . and led to the take-over of both houses of Congress by the Democrats for the first time since 1994.

The Iraq Study Group report, released in December, did little to settle the controversy over Iraq policy. Democrats and some Republicans hailed the proposals to pull back and redeploy US troops and prepare for withdrawal by 2008, but conservatives called it a surrender document. The Iraqis objected to the focus on an exit strategy without preventing civil war as well as the recommendation to privatize their oil industry.

Instead, Bush opted for the opposite policy, a large, sustained "surge" of US forces to increase security in critical areas of Iraq, which had been suggested in a competing report from a conservative think tank.

Considering the unpopularity of the war and GOP losses in the midterms, Bush's decision was bold, to say the least. In the spirit of Admiral Farragut, he ordered over twenty thousand more soldiers to Iraq to provide additional security in Baghdad and Anbar Province and to gain time for a hoped-for national reconciliation.

Bush's surge policy was stoutly opposed by the Democrats, who were committed to bringing the war to an end. In April 2007 Congress passed a bill ordering troop withdrawals by October, which Bush vetoed.

By June surge operations had begun under Gen. David Petraeus, whose strategy of protecting and building relationships with the local population rather than killing insurgents started to show positive results. While American troops did the heavy lifting on the security end, the Iraqi parliament, in charge of a political solution, took August off for vacation.

As the surge began to achieve its objectives, Democrats acknowledged the military progress but argued that the political progress Bush promised had not been made, and they continued to call for withdrawal of American troops.

Comparisons to Vietnam never failed to surface. The problem isn't that we fail to remember the lessons of history, it's that sometimes we learn different lessons.

Meanwhile in Gaza, deadly battles broke out between the Hamas and Fatah factions of the Palestinian Authority, which governed the Gaza Strip and the West Bank, culminating in a take-over by the militant Islamist Hamas and the ousting of Mahmoud Abbas's Fatah from Gaza.

In Paris, the United Nation's panel on climate change issued a report with new alarms over "unequivocal" global warming . . .

. . . caused by rising levels of greenhouse gases from burning fossil fuels.

On the domestic front, the Post Office issued the first "Forever" stamp, which could be used for future mailings no matter what the first-class rate might rise to.

Gasoline prices, as usual, did not remain steady, embarking on another steep rise in 2007.

A mass shooting by a student at Virginia Tech, in which thirty-two died, reignited the intense debate over guns, gun laws, and mental-health treatment and led to the strengthening of the National Instant Background Check System.

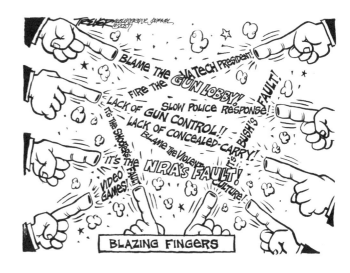

A major effort at a compromise immigration-reform bill, which would increase border security, create a guest worker program, and establish a path to legal status and citizenship for millions of illegal immigrants in the country, was attacked from both the left and the right and failed to reach a final vote in the Senate.

In sports, a massive report capping an investigation into the use of steroids and other performance-enhancing drugs in Major League Baseball was released . . .

Mirosław

... while other sports experienced doping, gambling, and criminal-behavior scandals.

2008 was dominated by two major stories: the financial crisis, which led to the Great Recession, and the election of Barack Obama. The financial crisis was precipitated by the "subprime crisis," which was in turn precipitated by the bursting of the housing bubble created by low interest rates, real-estate speculation, and mortgage lending to less credit-worthy borrowers.

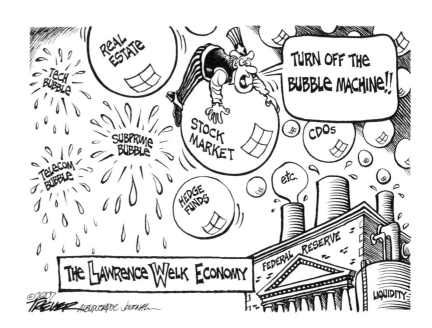

In the face of rising interest rates, home prices peaked in mid-2006 and began a rapid decline, which triggered defaults among many delinquent borrowers with adjustable-rate mortgages who found themselves unable to afford higher payments or refinance their loans. Many of these "subprime" mortgages had been bundled into mortgage-backed securities that were sold to investors and widely held. As these securities and various derivatives based on them lost value, credit markets around the world tightened, growth slowed, and recession loomed. The stock market began a plunge into a severe bear market.

In early 2008 the Federal Reserve warned of impending recession, and Congress quickly passed an economic stimulus package, which included tax rebates to low- and middle-income taxpayers. But the falling home prices began to threaten the viability of numerous financial institutions invested in mortgage-backed securities, including Bear Stearns, which had to be rescued by the Fed and the Bush administration.

As the credit markets continued to deteriorate, mortgage-lender Countrywide Financial collapsed and was taken over by the government, which then had to assume control of "mortgage giants" Fannie Mae and Freddie Mac, guarantors of 80 percent of the nation's home mortgages.

Meanwhile, in the 2008 presidential election primaries, Arizona Senator John McCain secured the Republican nomination by March. He was a strong supporter of the Iraq War and the Surge, but he didn't appeal to some of the more conservative elements of the party.

THE OLD MAN AND THE BLIND ELEPHANTS

Bush endorsed McCain, but, given the president's unpopularity, the two didn't campaign together, nor did Bush attend the GOP convention.

On the Democratic Party side, the leading candidates were all vocal opponents of the Iraq War, with Barack Obama the earliest and strongest foe.

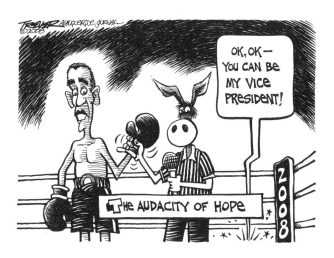

Senator Obama, who had written a book entitled *The Audacity of Hope* two years earlier, won the Iowa caucuses and surged in the polls, but Hillary Clinton eked out a victory in the New Hampshire primary. After the "Super Tuesday" primaries, with Clinton behind by only a few delegates, Obama shot down suggestions from the Clinton camp that a ticket with Obama as vice president would be "unstoppable."

With Obama winning the most states but Clinton taking the bigger states, the hard-fought race continued for three more months, until Obama finally secured the nomination in early June.

Despite expectations that Clinton would be considered for vice president, Obama decided on longtime Delaware senator Joe Biden, for his foreign-policy experience.

After months of record-setting fundraising, Obama reneged on an earlier commitment to accept public financing for the general election, the first major-party candidate to do so.

Leading up to the 2008 Summer Olympics in Beijing, there were protests and calls for boycotts over China's violations of free speech and human rights, particularly in Tibet, as well as the forced removal of poor Chinese to make room for Olympic venues.

In addition, there were major concerns over Beijing's air quality, the arrest and removal of dissidents from the city, suppression of negative news, and restrictions on internet access and journalists, giving a whole new meaning to the Olympic motto.

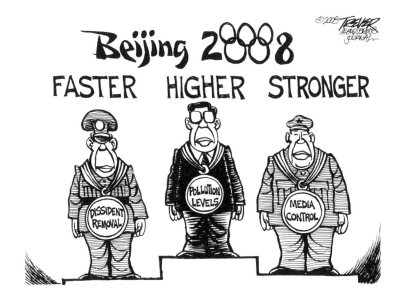

As the Olympics began, Russian forces invaded the former Soviet republic of Georgia, which had a pro-Western government after the

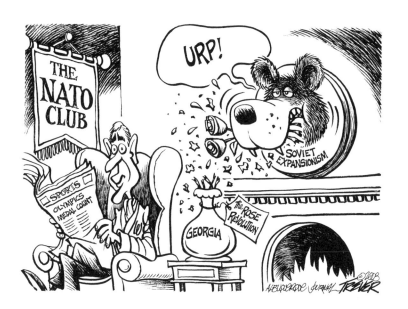

"Rose Revolution" of 2003. Bush had proposed NATO membership for Georgia in early 2008, which Putin termed a threat to Russian security. When fighting broke out between Georgian and separatist forces in two pro-Russian provinces, Russian troops launched a "peace enforcement" . . .

. . . bombing the capital of Tbilisi and pushing past the pro-Russian areas, occupying the cities of Gori and Poti in Georgia. Despite a negotiated cease fire, the fighting and destruction continued until the Russian troops pulled back a week later.

After the Georgia invasion, the United States and Poland announced a plan to place an anti-missile system in Poland as part of a NATO missile-defense shield. The Russians threatened a new arms race.

Just prior to the Republican convention, John McCain, hoping to allay concerns about his age, selected forty-four-year-old Alaska governor and "hockey mom" Sarah Palin to be his running mate. Having grown up hunting with her father and learning to "field-dress a moose," Palin electrified the conservative faithful with her acceptance speech.

As the 2008 campaign entered the home stretch, McCain's age and experience, coupled with Palin's youth and inexperience, faced off against Obama's promise of change, coupled with Biden's old-time Democrat politics.

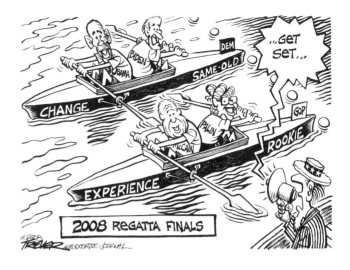

The subprime crisis continued to take its toll, with the Fed stepping in to rescue several major financial firms from bankruptcy, such as AIG. But the decision not to bail out Lehman Brothers, an investment bank heavily involved in risky mortgage securities, intensified the crisis.

With the credit markets freezing up and the global financial system reportedly on the brink of collapse, Treasury Secretary Henry Paulson proposed and Congress eventually passed a $700 billion rescue plan, called the Troubled Asset Relief Program (TARP), to restore liquidity to the system.

The idea that some institutions were so big and important to the economy that they couldn't be allowed to fail had its critics, who felt that such guarantees enabled these firms to profit from riskier behavior.

With the presidential race essentially even after a post-convention "bump" for the Republican ticket, McCain's reaction to the stock market crash following the Lehman bankruptcy was dramatic but erratic. After first calling the economic fundamentals "strong" and criticizing Wall Street, he suspended his campaign to return to Washington to help broker a bailout deal for Wall Street, which initially failed. He also decided to participate in the first Presidential debate after initially calling for a postponement. "No-drama" Obama's reaction was seen as calmer, as he declined to postpone the debate and found the crisis playing into his theme of the need for change.

Enjoying a fundraising advantage and good performances in all three presidential debates, Obama's lead widened in the polls and he won a convincing victory on election day. To commemorate Obama's win, I replaced the zeros in the White House's Pennsylvania Avenue address with his ubiquitous circular logo . . .

. . . Not ubiquitous enough, however, as a number of readers apparently didn't recognize the logo and were confused by the cartoon. (That's one of the risks of captionless cartoons.) I depicted the end of George W. Bush's presidency as book-ended by two great disasters, the 9/11 attacks and the 2008 financial crisis.

The impact of the recession in rapidly declining economic opportunity could be seen in the significant drop-off in immigration.

As 2008 drew to a close, the economic TARP package was stabilizing the financial markets, but the economy was officially in a deep recession, with no end in sight.

One of the Bush administration's last actions was to provide TARP funds to the US automobile industry, which was on the verge of bankruptcy from plummeting auto sales due to the consumer-credit crunch, high fuel prices rendering the profitable SUVs and pickup trucks less attractive, and foreign competition from producers of smaller, more fuel-efficient cars.

Several months later the government provided another bailout and assumed temporary control of General Motors and Chrysler, requiring them to go through a bankruptcy reorganization, facilitating cuts in labor costs and facilities. When the two exited bankruptcy in mid-2009, Chrysler was merged with Fiat and the government owned 61 percent of GM.

The new Obama administration also instituted new fuel-economy standards to reduce fuel consumption and greenhouse-gas emissions.

Upon taking office, Barack Obama moved quickly to pass an $800 billion stimulus plan to "jumpstart the economy" and save jobs, featuring tax relief, state and local fiscal support, and hefty spending programs on infrastructure projects, unemployment benefits, green energy, scientific research, and more.

The Japanese economy, mired in recurring recessions since 1990, however, was not an inspiring example.

Billed as the largest economic-recovery program in history, the stimulus was supposed to keep unemployment below 8 percent and spark a strong recovery. But unemployment continued to climb, and the plan was criticized for trying to do too much and spreading the money too thin.

While the recession officially ended in June 2009, the recovery was much slower and weaker than past recoveries from steep recessions. Much of the tax relief was doled out in small boosts to paychecks with little effect on consumer spending, while infrastructure projects, burdened with bureaucratic procedures, proved not to be "shovel-ready."

Obama then turned to promoting health-care reform, one of his central campaign themes and top legislative priorities. Addressing a joint session of Congress, he offered broad outlines for a comprehensive insurance plan and urged lawmakers to work out the specifics and write the bill.

Obama wanted a plan that would expand coverage and control rapidly rising health-care costs, which he hoped would bring down the budget deficit. Congressional committees set to work on the massive effort, but the Congressional Budget Office's vetting of the initial House bill showed it would add to the deficit.

The House bills included a "public option" for a government-run insurance plan that would compete with private insurance. Many thought that if everyone was going to end up in government health care, Congress should be required to have the same plan as everyone else.

When lawmakers returned to their districts in August to hold town-hall meetings on health care, many were met by upset constituents confused about major health-care changes. There were also angry protests over the stimulus, the bank and auto industry bailouts, and the rising deficit.

Obama continued to campaign for health-care legislation, addressing another joint session of Congress in September.

Arguments over the bill's provisions drew intense lobbying from a multitude of interests.

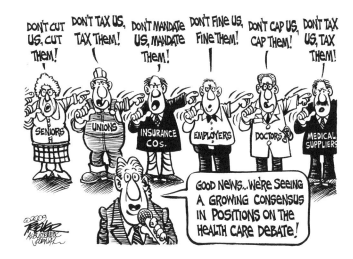

Meanwhile the economy continued to struggle as the unemployment rate topped 10 percent.

Obama signed an executive order
rescinding the Bush administration's constraints on embryonic
stem-cell research. At the same
time, as a favor to Nevada senator
Harry Reid, he killed funding for
the long-planned Yucca Mountain
repository for high-level nuclear
waste.

In a conciliatory speech in Cairo,
Obama called for a "new beginning" in relations with the Mus-
lim world, and he took his turn
at proposing a plan to end the
Palestinian-Israeli conflict.

In Afghanistan, Obama installed a
new commanding general and beefed
up the faltering war against the Taliban by sending more troops in pursuit of a strategy similar to the surge
in Iraq. Then he was awarded the
Nobel Peace Prize for "extraordinary
efforts to bring a new climate" to
international relations. In Oslo later
in the year, he acknowledged the
irony of accepting the award while
commander in chief of two wars.

In August, Sen. Ted Kennedy, long a leader in the battle for universal health care, died. Some Democrats hoped the outpouring of sympathy over his death would help pass the stalled health-care bill as a tribute to Kennedy.

Public opposition to Obamacare, as the bill came to be known, remained strong, however, and when a special election to fill Kennedy's Senate seat was won by a Republican, the Democrats lost their filibuster-proof sixty-seat majority. It took some fancy parliamentary maneuvering, with the House passing the Senate bill and then getting its budget-related changes passed via the reconciliation process (requiring only a majority vote), for the Democrats to ram their health-care bill through without a single Republican vote.

At the signing ceremony for the landmark legislation, Vice President Joe Biden was overheard getting a little over-exuberant.

Meanwhile, in its controversial *Citizens United* decision, the Supreme Court ruled that the First Amendment prohibits government restrictions on political speech by corporations, labor unions, and other groups, paving the way for a huge increase in independent expenditures in election campaigns.

In a campaign for the Senate, a Connecticut politician falsely claimed to have served in Vietnam.

A BP offshore oil platform in the Gulf of Mexico experienced a massive blowout, causing the largest marine oil spill in history.

The movement to legalize same-sex marriage gained momentum.

With the Republicans united in opposition to Obama initiatives but powerless in the minority, the 2010 midterm election season was dominated by public anger over the government bailouts, record deficits, and sweeping new health-care changes that focused mostly on the Democrats . . .

. . . who were further burdened by the slow economic recovery with lingering high unemployment.

The emergence of the anti-big-government Tea Party was a major boost to the Republicans, except for some moderate incumbents and "RINOs" (Republicans In Name Only) beaten in primary races by more conservative candidates enjoying Tea Party support.

Obama and the Democrats suffered a serious setback in the November midterms as the GOP retook control of the House and gained several Senate seats, governorships, and statehouses.

North Korean dictator Kim Jong Il died and was succeeded by his son, Kim Jong Un.

In Japan a 9.0 magnitude earthquake and ensuing tsunami damaged the Fukushima nuclear power plant, leading to core meltdowns and release of radioactivity into the air and sea. It was the worst nuclear accident since the 1986 Chernobyl disaster, further damaging confidence in nuclear power despite its lack of greenhouse-gas emissions.

As 2010 ended, after thirty-four years at the Journal and wishing to "slow down," I retired from daily editorial cartooning and limited my efforts to a weekly cartoon. At the same time, I ended my national syndication with King Features to focus on New Mexico subjects for the Sunday Journal. Since New Mexico politics rarely become a national story, almost all of my cartoons over the last decade have been on local concerns, as can be seen in chapter 7. However, there have been a few instances when the national scene proved irresistible, or when there was an overlap between national and state issues, and what follows are a few of my favorites.

Public-opinion polls showed the poor economic recovery was contributing to Obama's disapproval ratings exceeding his approval, but the GOP "do-nothing" Congress fared even worse.

Obama managed to win reelection in November 2012, with the Republicans retaining control in the House and Democrats in the Senate.

In 2014 the Veteran's Administration became embroiled in a scandal involving excessive wait times for veterans to get appointments and receive care at understaffed VA hospitals, including Albuquerque's. There were charges of falsified records to hide the wait times as well as over fifty patients dying in Phoenix before they were seen.

Former New Mexico governor Gary Johnson, who had been the Libertarian Party's candidate for president in 2012, when he won about 1 percent of the vote, decided to run again in 2016.

The Democrats would nominate Hillary Clinton, Obama's former Secretary of State and the first woman to head a major party ticket, while New York businessman, former reality TV show host, and outspoken outsider Donald Trump was the winner in a large Republican primary field. Johnson hoped to join the major party candidates in the presidential debates but was unable to reach the required 15 percent threshold in the polls.

A consistent leader in opinion surveys, Hillary Clinton was upset by Donald Trump, the most wildly popular or widely reviled candidate, depending on who you asked. Gary Johnson received 4.5 million votes—3.3 percent of the total and 9 percent in New Mexico—the most successful showing ever for the Libertarians.

Trump's immigration policies, including a border wall and "zero tolerance" for immigrants crossing the border illegally, led to outcries over family separations. Democrats argued for executive action to relieve the problem, while Republicans pushed for a more comprehensive immigration reform . . .

... a deadlock that persisted through the summer of 2019 and which saw caravans of asylum-seekers from Central America entering the country.

Trump's abrasive style and the radical reaction of the "Resistance" aggravated the partisanship and ideological divide, increasingly polarizing the country.

Then, as 2020 began, a deadly coronavirus broke out in Wuhan, China, and quickly spread into a worldwide pandemic. In the United States a national health emergency was declared, and, in an effort to "flatten the curve" of virus cases and to avoid overwhelming hospitals, the government ordered schools and "non-essential" businesses to be closed, leading to the worst economic decline since the Depression, with skyrocketing unemployment.

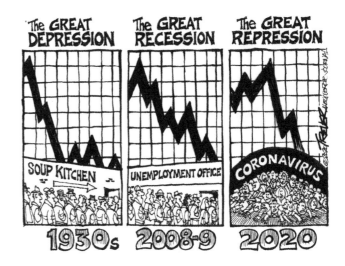

While the federal government spent trillions to alleviate the distress, citizens were asked to avoid large groups, wear masks, maintain "social distance," and stay home and "shelter in place." The "new normal" was very abnormal . . .

6. Joy of New Mexico

About half of the nine thousand–plus editorial cartoons I've drawn since 1976 have been devoted to New Mexico. Our state's climate and landscape are indeed enchanting, but the political climate and landscape are often less so, which provides ample opportunities for graphic satire. I like to point out that while our high desert location may suffer from a lack of precipitation in many years, there never seems to be a drought of cartoon material. Or that the only thing keeping pace with the fracking boom in the Permian Basin is the gusher of cartoon gold emanating from the Roundhouse in Santa Fe, Albuquerque's City Hall, the Bernalillo County Commission, and numerous other locales around the state.

New Mexico has some unique attributes that can be useful for a cartoonist. For instance, the rest of America is sometimes unsure whether we're really part of the United States. This has been a source of amusement and frustration for New Mexicans. *New Mexico Magazine* has a monthly feature devoted to this confusion among citizens of the other forty-nine states. The occasion of the seventy-fifth anniversary of New Mexico's statehood in 1987 provided a nice opportunity to add to the fun.

Years later, our geographically challenged fellow citizens came to mind again when, in the wake of 9/11, enhanced airport-security measures meant your regular New Mexico driver's license would no longer be accepted for boarding a plane.

"THERE GOES ANOTHER TON OF ENCHANTMENT."

New Mexico's nickname, "Land of Enchantment," reflecting its luminous landscape and unique cultural history, can also be a useful catch phrase.

Or, as in this instance, it can be handy in commenting on the problem of young people leaving the state due to lack of suitable opportunities.

One of the best things about cartooning in New Mexico is that we have a nontraditional state capitol, the Roundhouse. No typical building with a cliché dome like the US Capitol for us! Cartoonists are always on the lookout for unique visual images they can incorporate into a cartoon. The circular shape of our capitol makes it particularly useful. One of my first transformations of the Roundhouse was in this 1977 cartoon spoofing the power of the liquor interests in the Legislature.

"Listen, Bruce, the liquor license system is FINE the way it is. Now what's all this nonsense about ENFORCING it?"

Back in the 1980s, when the Legislature was having a debate over expanding commercial gambling in the state, the Roundhouse became a roulette wheel.

March 17, 1987.

Later it assumed the shape of a flip-top waste can. That's former Republican Governor Gary Johnson, submitting his agenda to a hostile Democratic legislature.

Over the years, in the course of making a point, I've converted the Roundhouse into a wishing well, an ash tray, a snail shell, a tire swing, a slot machine, a cyclotron, a unicycle, a steamroller, a curling stone, and many more. Here's the state capitol as the stone in the Greek myth of Sisyphus, with former Governor Susana Martinez, at the start of another legislative session, once more trying to roll it up the hill.

One last example depicts the Roundhouse as a wheel of loophole-ridden Swiss cheese to make a commentary on tax-reform politics.

The Roundhouse design, of course, is based on the sun symbol of the Zia Pueblo, featured on our number-one-rated state flag. Occasionally the Zia symbol itself has proven to be a convenient cartoon device. This cartoon was drawn during one of the state's recurrent budget crunches several years ago.

One of our unfortunately too-frequent
instances of political corruption in New
Mexico inspired this use of the Zia.

Then there was this example from the 2010
gubernatorial campaign, when Susana
Martinez and Diane Denish both won their
major party primaries. For the first time we
would elect a female governor, which was
an opportunity to make a small alteration
to the state flag.

Another iconic image associated with New Mexico is the hot-air balloon,
which I've used in many cartoons. My first experience with hot-air balloons came one morning in early October of 1976, shortly after I was hired
by the *Journal*. I was driving my family down I-25 from Denver to look for
a place to rent, and as we passed Bernalillo and neared Albuquerque, we
saw some mysterious, colorful shapes looming over a hill in the distance.

As we got closer, they turned out to
be hot-air balloons—we were driving past a mass ascension! It was our
first encounter with the annual Albuquerque International Balloon Fiesta,
which had begun only four years
earlier. It is one of New Mexico's signature events, and the hot-air balloon
would often provide me with a useful
metaphor. Most recently I used the
"mass ascension" to comment on the
burst of state spending made possible
by the fracking boom in southeast
New Mexico.

Just about every year, especially during "Balloon Week," at least one of my cartoons has featured a balloon. A popular event often held during the Fiesta is the "Key Grab," in which balloonists will launch at a distance away from the field and try to maneuver onto the field, close enough to grab the keys to a new vehicle off a tall pole. In 2013 this provided the setting for Albuquerque's mayoral election, conveniently held during Balloon Week . . .

. . . and won by Mayor Richard Berry, a notably "low-key" politician. Another event usually held during the Balloon Fiesta is a long-distance gas-balloon race. Gas balloons are featured in this cartoon from 1989, commenting on a period of forced budget-cutting by the Albuquerque Public Schools system.

"THE GOOD NEWS IS WE'RE GAINING ALTITUDE ... THE BAD NEWS IS WE'RE RUNNING OUT OF MUSIC TEACHERS AND LIBRARIANS...."

Smokey Bear is yet another famous New Mexico product. Rescued as a cub from a forest fire in the Capitan Mountains in 1950, Smokey was transferred to the National Zoo in Washington, DC, and became the living symbol for the US Forest Service's public-service advertising campaign for forest-fire prevention. In the 1990s, when its long-time policy of fire suppression was blamed for causing more destructive forest fires, the Forest Service began a program of "controlled burns" to reduce the build-up of accumulating deadwood, inspiring this depiction of a confused Smokey.

On the occasion of Smokey's sixty-fifth birthday, I pictured him in retirement.

Recently Smokey returned during a controversy over whether forest thinning and prescribed burns were endangering the habitat of the threatened Mexican spotted owl.

Finally, I should mention chile, New Mexico's iconic food staple, which has featured in a number of my cartoons and is one of the state's leading cash crops. In the 1980s Congressman Manuel Lujan proposed chile (that's *chile* with an *e*, not two *i*'s, if you please) for our official national food. Chile is either served green, when it is harvested earlier, or red, after it has ripened and been harvested later, so restaurant patrons are regularly asked which they prefer, a practice so ubiquitous that in 1999 the Legislature adopted "Red or Green?" as the official State Question, an occasional inspiration for a cartoon such as this one.

Whether customers want their chile hot or mild led to this cartoon when "concealed carry" of firearms in private establishments became legal.

New Mexico prides itself on producing the world's best chiles, and recently, when Colorado's governor claimed their green chiles were best, our governor, Michelle Lujan Grisham, quickly jumped to Hatch green chile's defense.

These are a few of the unique features that have made New Mexico such an enchanting environment for cartooning. My 2007 collection, *Mañana Republic*, was devoted entirely to my favorite cartoons about the state and its politics. The next chapter will catch you up on New Mexico happenings since then.

7. Bill, Susana, and Michele

New Mexico Governor Bill Richardson, who had easily won reelection to a second term in 2006, had spent much of that campaign season out of state laying the groundwork for a presidential bid. He finally announced his long-expected intentions in January with the formation of an "exploratory" committee to assess his chances. He faced a couple of obstacles, including a large field of candidates hoping to succeed President George W. Bush . . .

. . . and the need to finance his campaign by raising sufficient funds, to which end he generated some publicity by setting a record for shaking hands.

After four months of "exploring," to no one's surprise, Richardson made official his run for the presidency.

Campaigning in the early primary states as the first Hispanic to mount a nationwide campaign, he issued a series of position papers in hopes of attracting support.

By the fall he was polling just above 10 percent, but he remained firmly stuck behind the front-runners.

Meanwhile, six-term Republican senator Pete Domenici announced he wouldn't run again, much to the detriment of the Republicans' already dim prospects.

The open Senate seat attracted a significant roster of aspirants—the entire New Mexico congressional delegation: Republicans Heather Wilson and Steve Pearce, plus Democrat Tom Udall.

In other news, despite some favorable health statistics, New Mexico struggled with a doctor shortage, particularly in rural areas . . .

. . . as well as, apparently, not enough spending on health care.

Though slower-growing than its neighbors, the state's population rose to two million . . .

. . . while water supplies dropped amid alarms over global warming.

By the time the voting for president began in 2008, Richardson had fallen in the polls. He finished a distant fourth in the Iowa caucuses and headed for New Hampshire . . .

. . . where he again finished fourth, far behind Hillary Clinton, Barack Obama, and John Edwards. He immediately withdrew from the campaign and headed back to New Mexico.

Richardson, as an important Hispanic figure nationally, quickly faced a dilemma: whether to endorse Obama or Clinton for the nomination. That contest was exceedingly close, and he had hopes of ultimately being tapped for either vice president or secretary of state.

Ironically, the New Mexico Democratic primary had been moved to early February, presumably to aid Richardson's campaign, but given the closeness of the Obama-Clinton battle for delegates, the usual primary date might have made more of a difference.

When Richardson, who had served under Bill Clinton as both UN ambassador and energy secretary, finally decided to back Obama, Clinton's team was outraged, with James Carville calling him a "Judas."

The state's Senate primary was still in June, and the battle between former Air Force veterans Wilson and Pearce for the Republican nomination was fierce, while Democrat Udall was cruising to an uncontested spot on the ballot.

Sen. Domenici came out in favor of Wilson, but it was too late to overcome Pearce's lead.

In November, Udall beat Pearce handily, and the Democrats won both Wilson's and Pearce's House seats, turning the state's congressional delegation totally "blue" for the first time since 1969.

In business news, the state's biggest utility, the Public Service Company of New Mexico (PNM), which had to overcome antitrust concerns in 1985 when it bought the Gas Company of New Mexico, announced it was selling the natural gas subsidiary, which took the creative name of "New Mexico Gas Company."

Richardson announced that innovative electric car company Tesla planned to build its first factory in New Mexico, but then Tesla backed out of the deal in favor of a site in California.

In Albuquerque, Eclipse Aviation, which had developed the Eclipse 500 very light jet for the business market, ran into financial problems, lost a major client, and laid off much of its workforce . . .

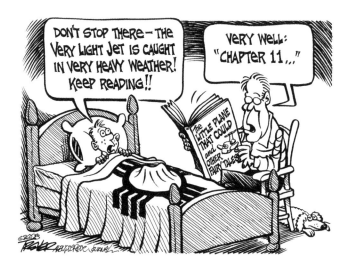

. . . and shortly thereafter declared bankruptcy.

Albuquerque Public Schools hired a new superintendent, Winston Brooks, former head of the Wichita school system, in hopes of raising low student proficiency levels to meet the federal No Child Left Behind goals.

Gov. Richardson's education plan included a proposal that students be required to get passing grades to get a driver's license.

Former Democratic state Senate president pro tem Manny Aragon was found guilty of conspiracy to siphon off over $4 million from the new Bernalillo County Metropolitan Courthouse construction project.

UNM alum and coach Rocky Long, after rebuilding the Lobo football program and taking it to five bowl games, resigned in frustration after one bad year.

Barack Obama won the 2008 Presidential election with Joe Biden as his running mate. Bill Richardson, claiming he was happy as governor, was still entertaining secretary of state hopes, given his experience as UN ambassador and in foreign prisoner-release negotiations. When that position went to Hillary Clinton, he was nominated for another cabinet post.

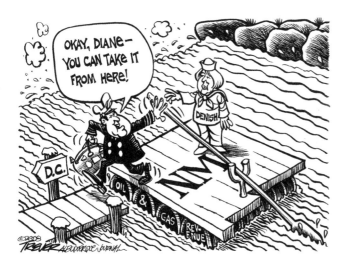

Richardson prepared to leave for Washington and handed the helm to Lieutenant Governor Diane Denish as the economy was about to plunge into the Great Recession.

But Richardson's nomination quickly ran into trouble when it was learned a federal grand jury was investigating "pay-to-play" allegations involving Richardson's state-infrastructure program. Saying the investigation would unduly delay the confirmation hearings, Richardson withdrew from consideration for the cabinet job.

Subsequent court proceedings revealed that lucrative contracts had been awarded to investment firms that had contributed to Richardson's political-action committees. All along, he denied any involvement in wrongdoing.

Later in the year, while Richardson was on a trade mission to Cuba, the US Justice Department decided not to pursue indictments in the case.

Nevertheless, intimations of scandal tarnished Richardson's reputation, weakening his command of state politics, and strengthened calls for ethics reform.

Lieutenant Governor Denish, hoping to succeed Richardson as governor but denied the chance to gain some incumbency, took steps to distance herself from him by supporting ethics reforms.

SEPARATION ANXIETY

During the 2009 Legislature, State Representative Janice Arnold-Jones set up a website and began live-streaming a committee meeting, forcing a debate on increasing government transparency and ultimately leading to the recording and archiving of legislative proceedings on the Legislature's website.

Meanwhile, the Legislature passed a law, signed by Richardson, to abolish capital punishment.

Richardson's tenure had been blessed so far with ample tax revenues, but with the onset of the Great Recession, budget problems loomed.

The passage of President Obama's stimulus program promised some relief.

In Albuquerque's "non-partisan" mayoral campaign, three-term incumbent Democrat Marty Chavez was challenged by Democrat Richard Romero and Republican Richard Berry.

Chavez touted the need for a modern rail transit system, which was immediately derided by his opponents.

Perhaps due to a bit of Marty-fatigue, Chavez lost his bid for a fourth term. Berry, avoiding a run-off by winning a 43 percent plurality, seized the leadership of "The Q," as the city is sometimes known.

Rocky Long's replacement, Mike Locksley, became embroiled in both on-field and off-field controversies, and led the UNM football team to a 1-11 record.

New Mexico's longest-serving governor, Bruce King, a popular politician with a ready smile and hearty handshake, who famously once mistook a roadrunner carving for a woodpecker, passed away.

The Great Recession affected New Mexico a bit later than the rest of the country, but by 2010 revenues had fallen further, and the state faced a $500 million shortfall. The influx of federal "stimulus" money was insufficient to close the gap, so the Legislature was faced with difficult choices.

The Senate favored spending cuts while the House wanted tax increases.

Gov. Richardson resisted cuts to the growing film-subsidy program, the state's new sacred cow.

Other levels of government were also suffering from budget shortfalls.

The public schools continued to receive low student academic achievement ratings . . .

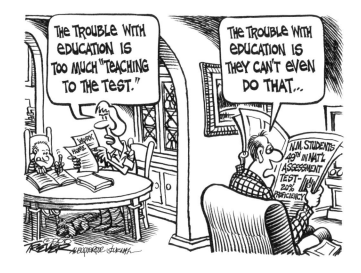

. . . which required many remedial courses for students in the state's proliferating system of branch colleges.

At Kirtland Air Force Base an ongoing leak from an underground jet-fuel tank was discovered, possibly threatening to contaminate water wells near the base.

I generally avoided using Chuck Jones's Roadrunner and Coyote characters in my cartoons, but in this case it was irresistible. Controversy over how to contain the leak and prevent further contamination would continue for years.

The New Mexico State Game Commission relaxed its bear-hunting limits.

After a year-long remodeling, UNM's famous basketball arena reopened to mixed reviews.

In June Democrat Lieutenant Governor Diane Denish and Republican Susana Martinez, the Doña Ana County District Attorney, had won their respective party primaries. As the fall campaign heated up, Denish found that the formerly popular Gov. Richardson was not providing the expected boost.

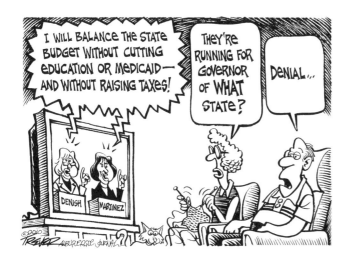

Both candidates promised plans to deal with the state's fiscal problems.

Bill Clinton campaigned for Denish, lampooning Martinez's Texas roots . . .

. . . but Martinez steadily increased her advantage in the polls and won comfortably in November to become New Mexico's first elected female governor and the nation's first Latina governor.

As Bill Richardson prepared to leave office, a yard sale was held to de-access some items accumulated after eight years in the Governor's Mansion.

While observers offered conflicting evaluations of his governorship, Richardson announced some future plans.

Susana Martinez moved into the Governor's office . . .

. . . and immediately had to declare a state of emergency when a record cold spell forced the New Mexico Gas Company, which was about to ask for a rate increase, to cut off service to thirty thousand customers when gas suppliers had to curtail production.

Martinez's push to repeal a state law allowing illegal immigrants to get New Mexico driver's licenses was opposed by the Democratic Legislature . . .

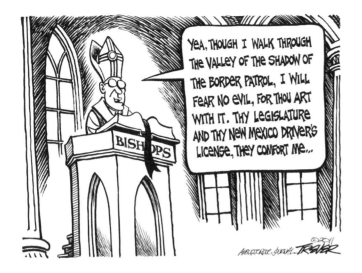

. . . as well as some in the religious community.

Martinez also wanted to cut subsidies to the film industry, but she compromised on a $50 million annual cap.

In other arts news, the New Mexico Symphony Orchestra declared bankruptcy, but from its ashes rose the new, trimmer New Mexico Philharmonic.

Martinez brought in Hanna Skandera from Florida Governor Jeb Bush's administration to spearhead education reforms. The teacher unions were not welcoming . . .

. . . but New Mexico's ranking in numerous educational surveys continued to show the need for change.

Unable to agree earlier with the governor on how to redraw legislative districts after the 2010 census, the Legislature reconvened for a special session in the fall.

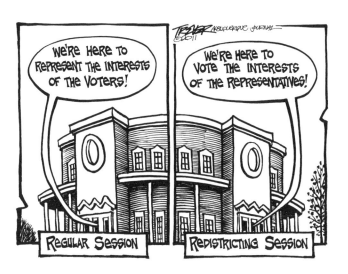

Once again Martinez vetoed the Democrats' plan and left it up to the courts to decide.

Republican Secretary of State Dianna Duran launched a massive investigation of possible voter fraud, but it turned up very few cases.

UNM hired a new football coach, Bob Davie, who had previously coached at Notre Dame.

Former governor Gary Johnson entered the race for the 2012 Republican presidential nomination, but he got no traction in the crowded field . . .

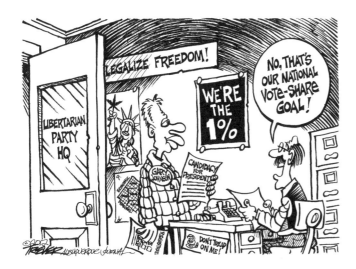

. . . so he switched to the Libertarian Party instead, with no guarantee of better visibility.

On January 6, 2012, New Mexico celebrated its statehood centennial.

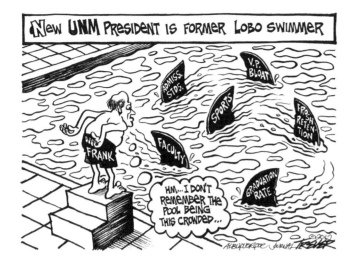

UNM, facing numerous challenges, selected a new president.

In the Roundhouse, the Democratic Legislature and the Republican Martinez faced off for another round of killing each other's legislative goals.

One of the casualties was Martinez's proposal to end "social promotion." Citing New Mexico's dismal reading-proficiency scores, the third-grade retention bill sought to hold back students not reading at grade level.

The overdose death rate from pre-
scription drugs began to exceed the
state's notoriously high rate from
illegal drugs.

US Senator Jeff Bingaman
announced he would not run for
a sixth term in 2012. With six-
term Sen. Pete Domenici leaving
only four years earlier, the loss
of seniority raised concerns as
looming federal budget cuts
threatened the national labs.

Congressman Martin Heinrich and
former Congresswoman Heather
Wilson battled to succeed Bingaman, wielding different energy
policies.

As Wilson continued to lag in the polls, campaign funds dried up, and Heinrich cruised to victory.

Sandoval County consolidated polling places, severely reducing those in Albuquerque's rapidly growing neighbor, Rio Rancho.

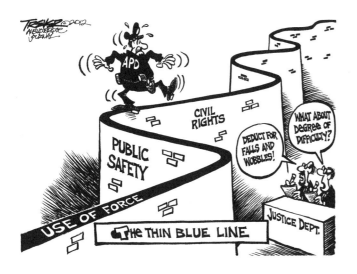

In the wake of a rising number of officer-involved shootings, the US Department of Justice began an investigation into the Albuquerque Police Department for a "pattern of excessive use of force," as APD tried to navigate between the demands of fighting crime and observing constitutional rights.

As 2013 kicked off and some New Mexicans celebrated by shooting firearms in the air, Martinez's agenda faced continued opposition.

In hopes that it might improve the state's dismal rankings in elementary and secondary student performance, New Mexico began phasing in state-wide full-day kindergarten in 2000. After a while, with little improvement, it was thought that expanded pre-kindergarten programs were needed. As the pressure for more comprehensive early-childhood services mounted, the idea that nothing could be improved until each preceding stage had improved inspired this cartoon with a classic "circle of blame" image.

Gov. Martinez and Education Chief Skandera began implementing a controversial system of public K-12 teacher evaluations emphasizing student improvement.

Teachers and their unions were fiercely opposed to the reforms and sued to stop them.

The state lottery was unable to continue fully funding the popular lottery scholarship program for college students due to rising college costs and a falloff in lottery receipts. I suggested a solution.

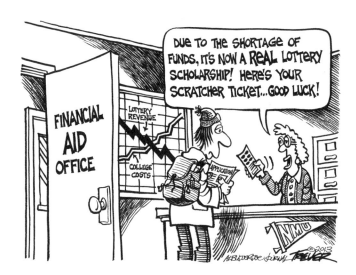

New Mexico's health-care system was under pressure from a chronic shortage of doctors and an increasing need for services.

New Mexico finished atop at least one ranking in 2013. Unfortunately, it was for the severest drought . . .

. . . which was then alleviated in typical monsoon fashion.

Despite solid public support for elements of her agenda, including third-grade retention and no driver's licenses for undocumented immigrants, the Roundhouse impasse mostly continued as New Mexico began the 2014 gubernatorial election year.

Near Carlsbad, an underground explosion caused the temporary closing of the Waste Isolation Pilot Plant. Subsequently we learned that containers of low-level radioactive materials shipped from Los Alamos had been improperly packed with nitrate waste and a moisture remover composed of—you can't make this up—kitty litter! Sometimes reality is stranger than cartoons.

Having lost out on the Tesla factory, New Mexico entertained thoughts of landing its newest megaproject with lower corporate taxes . . .

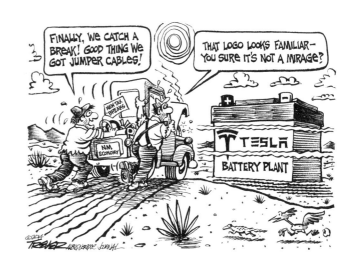

. . . and a huge incentive package, but big-time gambling mecca Nevada ultimately won the competition.

Gordon Eden was named chief of the Albuquerque Police Department, which was beset by understaffing, controversy over excessive "militarization," and public protests over recent high-profile police shootings . . .

. . . and his appointment was made just before the Department of Justice announced its finding that APD had "engaged in a pattern or practice of excessive force," which would require a comprehensive settlement agreement and court-supervised reforms to APD.

Meanwhile, the rapid growth in trade with Mexico was straining port-of-entry facilities on the southern border.

In the fall of 2014, a test flight of Virgin Galactic's SpaceShip Two craft ended in disaster as it broke apart and killed one of the pilots, a serious setback for New Mexico's Spaceport America's plans to host commercial suborbital space flights any time soon.

In the 2014 governor's race, Democratic Attorney General Gary King, son of former governor Bruce King, won a hard-fought primary while Martinez was unopposed. King's general-election campaign was severely underfunded . . .

. . . and the well-financed Republican Martinez cruised to an easy victory in November. In a real surprise, the Republicans won control of the state House of Representatives for the first time in sixty years.

The new state House majority, however, was unable to pass key parts of
the Republican agenda because the
still-Democratic state Senate refused
to agree.

The House and Senate failed to
pass the important capital outlay
bill with over $200 million in
public-works projects. A special
session of the Legislature was
needed, but continuing dis-
agreements over priorities and
financing delayed passage of the
package until June.

APD, now under federal monitoring,
struggled with depleted ranks . . .

. . . while the violent-crime rate continued to climb, including the killing of two police officers.

Efforts to reduce jail overcrowding, along with new bail and speedy-trial rules, led to early releases of offenders onto the streets to commit new crimes.

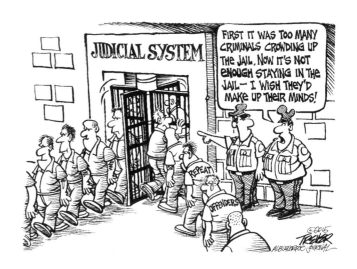

Republican Secretary of State Dianna Duran resigned and pled guilty to embezzlement of campaign funds to cover gambling expenses at local casinos.

Albuquerque's Mayor Berry announced the ART (Albuquerque Rapid Transit) project, an ambitious new public transportation effort with sixty-foot articulated electric buses, which reminded one of an earlier transit system.

Meanwhile, the Rail Runner was experiencing ridership declines and other problems.

While Amtrak considered rerouting its Southwest Chief passenger train away from Santa Fe and Albuquerque, an unprecedented plunge in states revenues, mostly due to oil and gas price declines . . .

... forced the Legislature to focus on shoring up finances and cutting spending.

The new ART project, which involved reducing traffic lanes and creating a bus-only center lane down Albuquerque's Central Avenue, was approved by City Council but drew strong opposition from local merchants whose businesses would be disrupted.

Progress on achieving required APD policing reforms being monitored by the US Department of Justice was mostly disappointing.

New Mexico's closed primary system continued to shut out independents.

Republican presidential candidate Donald Trump campaigned in Albuquerque.

Trump's anti-immigrant comments about "Mexican rapists" and his vow to build a Mexican border wall put fellow Republican Gov. Martinez in an awkward position.

In the November state elections, the Republicans succeeded in ousting a nemesis, state Senate Majority Leader Michael Sanchez, but they lost control of the House of Representatives.

Obtaining identification complying with the strict national security requirements of the REAL ID Act, which would be needed to board an airplane after October 2020, proved confusing for many drivers.

The year ended with another bleak revenue outlook.

With a Republican governor and the Democrats back in charge of both houses of the Legislature, chances for compromise were few, and the 2017 session quickly became contentious. The Legislature tackled a looming budget shortfall with a few spending cuts and large tax increases . . .

. . . which Martinez promptly vetoed, along with cutting the entire budget for the Legislature and higher education. The funding was restored in the ensuing special session, but the Democrats' second attempt at a tax-increase package was again vetoed.

The crime rate in Albuquerque continued to rise, with the criminal-justice system adopting rules for pre-trial release based on perceived risk to public safety rather than ability to pay . . .

. . . and upending the old bail-bond system.

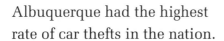

Albuquerque had the highest rate of car thefts in the nation.

A multi-agency task force was organized to tackle the problem.

The Pit celebrated its fiftieth anniversary, but declining attendance numbers were adding to the UNM Athletic Department's budget problems.

The state's guardianship system was rocked by a scandal involving embezzlement and other improper actions by guardians and conservators entrusted with the care and finances of people declared incapacitated and unable to care for themselves.

State auditor and former state senator Tim Keller was elected mayor of Albuquerque, despite some campaign donation irregularities.

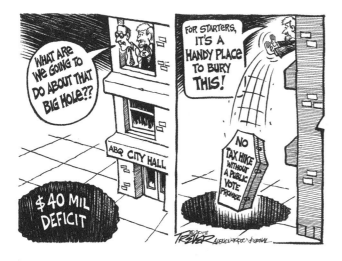

Despite a promise not to raise taxes without a public vote, Keller pointed to a projected budget deficit and the need to hire more police as reasons for rushing to pass a 3/8-cent gross-receipts tax increase.

Inheriting the problem-plagued ART bus system from the Berry administration and discovering numerous mechanical faults, safety issues, and construction deficiencies, Keller called the program "a bit of a lemon."

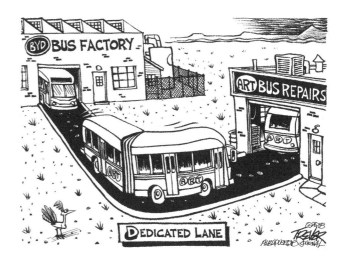

Keller ultimately rejected the faulty electric buses and ordered a new fleet of diesel buses from a different company.

The Albuquerque City Council passed a resolution strengthening its "immigrant-friendly" policy of not helping enforce federal immigration laws.

Early-childhood-services advocates continued to agitate for getting more money for their programs, without raising taxes, by tapping the fully dedicated Land-Grant Permanent Fund.

A state district judge issued a ruling that New Mexico was violating the constitutional right of students by not providing them an adequate education for college or career. While one might argue this was true for most New Mexico students, the decision focused on insufficient funding for at-risk students—children from low-income homes, English-language learners, Native Americans, and disabled students.

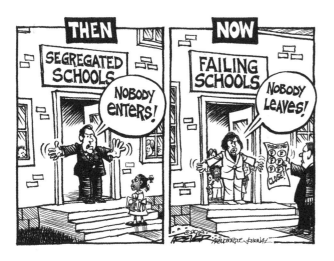

The Martinez administration's efforts to close some consistently low-performing schools, allowing students to transfer to better schools, was resisted by APS.

In an attempt to balance the athletic department's budget, UNM made the controversial decision to cut several sports, including the successful men's soccer program.

Albuquerque continued to struggle with its growing homeless problem.

On Wall Street the long bull market had a sharp sell-off, and the 2018 campaign for governor followed its usual course.

The November election was a "blue tsunami," with Michelle Lujan Grisham winning the governorship and Democrats sweeping all the statewide offices and congressional races and enlarging their majority in the state House.

Riding another tsunami, of revenues from oil and gas production, Lujan Grisham and the Legislature immediately set to work to enact their wish list . . .

. . . which included some major tax increases, notwithstanding the record revenue from fossil fuels . . .

. . . which they planned to phase out in favor of renewable energy sources in years to come.

Hoping to join the stampede of states legalizing the sale and production of marijuana, the Legislature passed a bill setting up a working group to develop a plan in time for a future Legislature.

Thousands of Central Americans, fleeing poverty and violence in their homeland, attempted to claim asylum in the United States, stressing border-patrol facilities. Some were temporarily housed on the State Fairgrounds.

President Trump held another rally in New Mexico, this time in Rio Rancho.

The Keller administration prematurely trumpeted favorable crime-rate statistics, only to have to amend the figures and backtrack.

The controversial and long-delayed ART system buses began running down their dedicated center lanes on Central Avenue. Immediately there were a series of collisions as unaware drivers attempted left turns across the center lanes.

When 2020's COVID-19 pandemic hit, Gov. Lujan Grisham declared a public-health emergency, banning large public gatherings and ordering schools and "non-essential" businesses to shut down, in hopes of avoiding a "tsunami" of coronavirus cases. The collateral damage to commerce, employment, and personal and public finances was severe.

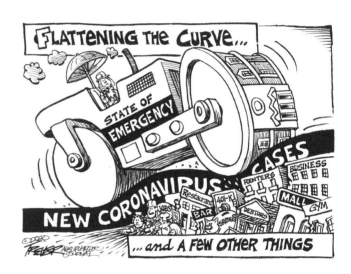

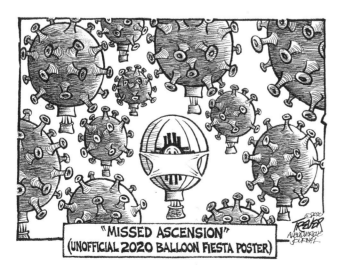

"MISSED ASCENSION" (UNOFFICIAL 2020 BALLOON FIESTA POSTER)

As the lockdown persisted, a tsunami of cancellations of major public events ensued, including the Santa Fe Opera, the State Fair, and the Albuquerque International Balloon Fiesta.

As some businesses prepared to reopen in the state, the killing of George Floyd in Minneapolis sparked nationwide protests, both peaceful and violent. The outrage quickly spread to Albuquerque, where a march against police brutality degenerated into rioting and vandalism against downtown buildings.

I dislike ending on a sour note, but the year was one of pandemic, isolation, loss, discord, and division for many. Perhaps the annual Zozobra burning in Santa Fe provided a catharsis.

8. *FAQ*

*A*fter several years with the *Journal* I began to get invitations to speak to various local groups, something I imagine happens to most cartoonists, as desperate program chairmen scrounge for what they hope will be entertaining speakers. In the ensuing decades I had the opportunity to address numerous civic, professional, and continuing-education groups as well as to visit school classes of all ages. Some cartoonists are adept at live sketching before an audience, but this wasn't my forte (and I rarely felt comfortable with it), but I usually brought along an oversized drawing pad for the elementary school classes and did some quick and simple sketches to engage their interest. Generally I would rely on slide presentations to entertain the larger and older gatherings. I would use a carousel projector to show twenty to thirty slides of my favorite cartoons along with a few one-liners and commentary on the current political scene and the nature of political cartooning. I relied on slides and the carousel projector for many years, until after I retired and was dragged into the digital age. In recent years I learned to put my cartoon images into PowerPoint and copy everything onto a thumb drive. I usually tended to over-prepare for my talks and have extensive notes so as not to forget a point or mess up a one-liner. But I always enjoyed the question period at the end, when I was able to relax and be extemporaneous in fielding the inevitable questions from the audience. What follows are a few of the most popular ones.

"How Do You Get Your Ideas?"

This is one of the first questions a cartoonist gets. My usual flippant answer is "I wish I knew—I'd get out of the office a lot sooner." I had some fun with a cartoonist's idea sources in this cartoon, drawn in response to a 1979 Supreme Court decision—*Herbert v. Lando*—that allowed investigation into a journalist's thought processes in order to dis-

"...A JOY BUZZER, TWO MAD MAGAZINES, THREE LOOSE SCREWS, SOME SILLY PUTTY, A BANANA PEEL,..."

cover possible malice in libel cases. But every cartoonist has some sort of procedure or routine that he or she goes through in search of inspiration. Many cartoonists are compulsive doodlers, constantly sketching and writing down thoughts. And more than a few of my fellow editorial cartoonists are in the habit of carrying a sketchbook and regularly caricaturing whomever is around them— good practice, I suppose, and sometimes entertaining.

I've never really been much of a doodler, even when I had a sketchbook with me, though I do carry a small spiral-bound notebook in case an idea suddenly hits. Unfortunately, that rarely happens. For me, it seems that cartoon ideas usually come from a more laborious process. I would start by reading the *Albuquerque Journal*, first with breakfast for pleasure (headlines, sports, and comics), then again later at the office to find a topic. Then I might peruse the office copies of the *Wall Street Journal* and the *New York Times*. In the late morning the first edition of the *Albuquerque Tribune* would arrive. I would keep reading, hoping that some situation, controversy, or quote would spark an idea. When all else failed—if there wasn't anything new in the "news" that day—there was always a nearby pile of rough sketches from previous days that hadn't made it into finished cartoons but could be easily resurrected.

In selecting a topic, I try to keep in mind that my audience is the readers of the *Albuquerque Journal* and that I'm drawing for them. I put myself in the position of Will Rogers: "All I know is what I read in the papers."

That means that my cartoons need to concern stories that have been in the paper, not what's on the TV news (although they're frequently the same, as the *Journal* has often set the agenda for local coverage). Cartoonists aren't reporters. We don't "break the news," we react to it. So we need the readers to at least be somewhat aware of the story we're cartooning about.

Life would have been simpler if I just selected the subject of the next day's editorial to draw about, but that rarely happened. In the morning editorial meeting we would toss around topics, debating what positions we should take but usually not making firm determinations on which editorials would run the next day. Because I often needed to commit to a drawing before that decision was made, we rarely coordinated. Naturally I preferred the freedom to choose the topic that, in my opinion, would make the best cartoon. In recent years, after I downshifted to doing only a Sunday cartoon and the editors began deciding on the Sunday topic earlier in the week, I've sometimes been able to craft a suitable cartoon to go along with the editorial.

Once having decided on a topic and the angle I would take on it, it was time to do some brainstorming to get a workable idea and then come up with a means of conveying it. Since brevity is the soul of wit, as Shakespeare would have it, the cartoonist looks for an image that concisely expresses his conception of an issue. Some cartoonists call this their "vehicle," but I prefer the term "visual metaphor." I start to compile a list of images, words, phrases, quotes, jokes, clichés, and so on that relate somehow to the issue until something finally clicks, and an idea emerges. In the past I've created long lists of these references, compiling them on notecards and scrap paper and keeping them in folders of recurring topics for future use. One of the mottos in this business is, "Never throw anything away." Occasionally I've even brought in a whole separate topic as a means of commenting on the original topic, what my current editor calls a "twofer."

There are days that the news provides many possibilities for a good cartoon, and the problem is settling on one. When the headlines are full of crisis, controversy, and revolting developments, friends and colleagues have often exclaimed to me, "Boy, you must be having a field day right now!" (In recent years, during the Era of Trump, I got that a lot. Unfortunately, I was only doing local cartoons then.) And then there are days when topics are few and uninspiring, and the problem is getting the proverbial blood from a stone. As the deadline for filling that empty space on the editorial page approached, and a blank drawing pad stared back at me, I would take the least-bad idea of an unpromising lot and hope the drawing would carry the day. To mangle an old song lyric, "If you're not drawing the cartoon you love, love the one you're drawing."

"Does the *Journal* Tell You What to Draw?"

This is another common question. While that might shorten my workday, I can honestly say that I've never been asked to toe the editorial line at the *Journal*. Most cartoonists would prefer to be treated like syndicated columnists, who are published whether or not they mirror the opinions of the newspaper. While more often than not my views have been similar to the *Journal*'s, there have been times when my cartoons did not agree with the editorials. Most notable was the time in 1982 when Sen. Jack Schmitt was running for reelection and ran some ads against his challenger Jeff Bingaman, which took liberties with the truth.

This cartoon ran on the same day that the *Journal* endorsed Schmitt.

I feel lucky that I've been granted a good deal of independence at the *Journal*. In forty-plus years with the paper and more than nine thousand cartoons, I've probably had fewer than a dozen "killed" and not published—and this never happened over political differences. Usually it would be over a matter of taste—cartoonists are frequently accused by upset readers of lacking it—or a late-breaking event that rendered the cartoon moot or easily misconstrued, such as the time my cartoon employing an airplane image had to be pulled when there was an overnight plane-crash tragedy.

"A MR. SCHMITT TO see YOU, DOCTOR— CLAIMS IT'S AN eMeRGeNCY,..."

This is not to say I never heeded the editors or asked for their advice. In order to avoid having a finished cartoon killed or changed, early on I sought my editor's feedback on what I planned to draw. Sometimes I just had a single idea in a rough drawing to show the editorial-page editor and get an okay to go ahead. At other times I had several roughs that I'd present to get an opinion on which was the best or timeliest. And often they'd ask which one was *my* favorite and then tell me to go ahead with it.

My fellow editorial cartoonists around the country did not always experience the gentle editorial hand I enjoyed, however. At the annual convention of the Association of American Editorial Cartoonists, many would gripe about all the cartoons they had had killed or "spiked" over differences with their editors. In fact, several years ago the AAEC instituted a "Golden Spike Award" for the best cartoon that had met this fate.

Obviously my slant in a cartoon could be influenced by *Journal* editorial positions, particularly on local issues, but I also relied on various other resources. In addition to the *New York Times* and the *Wall Street Journal*, such sources might include magazines I subscribed to, such as *Newsweek* or *National Review*. Despite the advent of cable TV and the internet, I've stubbornly stuck to print journalism for most of my information. For additional background I have kept extensive files of stories on various local and national topics that I've clipped or photocopied and which I stuffed into several file cabinets in my office. These files also included a multitude of pictures of everything from flora and fauna to trains, planes, automobiles, and much more—the artist's "morgue," as it's called—which I could use for reference to help with a drawing. Naturally, I also kept folders full of photos and caricatures of all the state and national politicians I had occasion to draw.

"Do You Ever Get Death Threats?"

Those who suspect that my opinions might not always be welcomed by some readers ask me this question. Fortunately I can answer "no" to that, although I did get a call once from a gentleman who wanted to "punch me out" for that morning's cartoon. I tried not to be nasty or malicious in my work, but I was certainly not immune to phone calls or letters to the editor objecting to my views on an issue. I also, less frequently, would get calls from readers thanking me for a cartoon that had agreed with their views.

I think I was only picketed once, when a local activist group took umbrage at a cartoon I did lampooning their demands on an issue involving the local Intel factory. About a dozen of the group trooped into the newsroom (these were the days before tighter security), paraded around with signs and singing a protest song, and then presented me with a new box of crayons—no threats, just good, albeit sarcastic, fun. Another group demanded a meeting with the editorial board to protest a cartoon I'd done on the latest search for a new UNM president, but after a few tense moments it became a very civil exchange of views. Then there was the day that a couple of gentlemen from the Albuquerque Police Department came into the office and asked to see me. It seemed they were upset because I had used McGruff the Crime Dog and his "Take a bite out of crime" slogan in a cartoon on a local police matter. They were there to inform me that I was misappropriating a trademarked character, but I insisted that this was an instance of "fair use" in copyright law, established in several cases such as the Reddy Kilowatt decision, which upheld the right of environmental groups and cartoonists to satirize the character.

But you can never predict how some readers will react. One day I drew a non-political cartoon about the 1998 home-run race between Mark McGwire and Sammy Sosa. I put their faces, along with those of Babe Ruth and Roger Maris, into a Mount Rushmore configuration and called it "Mount Crushmore," a somewhat lame pun, I'll admit. A lady wrote in to complain about "the cartoon in the paper" that day, and after an exchange of letters it was determined it was my cartoon, and not another on the page, that was the problem. It turned out that she believed it was inappropriate, even sacrilegious, to use a revered national monument in such a way. I didn't have the heart to tell her that I had taken liberties with Mt. Rushmore in several previous cartoons, as have many other cartoonists, and I have done so with other icons like the Statue of Liberty. Instead I just put the incident into the "you never know" file.

"Do You Take Ideas and Suggestions from Outside Sources?"

Occasionally I've been asked this one. Yes, readers do call up and say they have a "great idea" for a cartoon, but they can't draw, and they hope that I'll sketch it for a cartoon in the paper. Generally I thank them for calling and being a reader and tell them that I'll "put it in the hopper" for consideration. Unfortunately, I'm almost never able to use these suggestions. Maybe they're not on a topic that's timely or that I'm currently interested in, or maybe it's too complicated to put into a cartoon. Often they don't fit my style or sense of humor, or I don't share their opinion about an issue. I do take some pride in generating all my own cartoon ideas, but I am always willing to listen, since while a reader's idea might not quite work as presented, it might suggest another idea to me. One of the rare times I used an idea as suggested was in this cartoon about government over-regulation, the idea for which was provided by my late uncle—we had similar senses of humor.

"Do You Have a Political Philosophy?"

This is another question I'm sometimes asked. My answer is yes, I've always thought it important for a political cartoonist to have a basic philosophy or framework to which he can relate the day's events. It helps him to avoid being untethered and scattershot in his opinions and also prevents him from being rigid or doctrinaire. A healthy skepticism about politics and government is a good starting point. I wasn't trained as a journalist, but I believe in the old maxim, "If your mother says she loves you, check it out." As a cartoonist, I always liked Mark Twain's quip, "Get your facts first, you can distort them later." To nail down those facts, of course, I have relied totally on, and was always grateful for, the diligent efforts of the writers and editors who researched and produced the stories on which I based my cartoons.

My own political preferences developed over the course of many years. I grew up in the 1950s, a time heavily impacted by the Cold War and anti-communism. The media, in the wake of the Depression and World War II, were mostly dominated by liberal ideas then, with a bias toward government action to solve problems. Early on, of course, I was influenced by my parents, who I think were Eisenhower Republicans on most issues, except for some liberal leanings on foreign policy. In college I wasn't really that interested in politics, but I suppose I leaned moderate, as a liberal Republican (when that was not an oxymoron). In the turbulence of the 1960s I was a bit like a cork in stormy seas, bouncing around from favoring Johnson over Goldwater and Nixon over Humphrey, in favor of civil rights but not affirmative action, for desegregation but against forced busing, for fighting communism but maybe not in Vietnam. In graduate school I became a fan of Milton Friedman's free-market economics, as expressed in *Capitalism and Freedom*, as well as Hans Morgenthau's ideas of realism in foreign policy. I also began subscribing to *National Review* to get familiar with conservative arguments.

Early in my cartooning career I would call myself a libertarian conservative. The Libertarian Party was founded in Colorado in 1971, shortly before I moved to Denver, and it was actually on the Colorado ballot in 1972, providing an alternative to Nixon and George McGovern. I was exposed to several libertarian writers, such as Albert Jay Nock, Harry Browne, and Murray Rothbard, and I became interested in the Austrian School economists, including Ludwig Von Mises and Henry Hazlitt. Particularly influential was Friedrich Hayek's *The Road to Serfdom*.

Elaborating on the standard one-dimensional Left-Right / Liberal-Conservative continuum, the Libertarians had developed a two-dimensional grid to express more nuanced differences in politics:

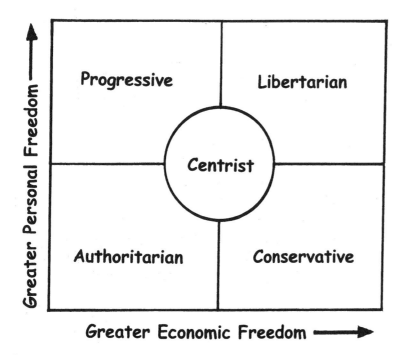

With Economic Freedom on one axis and Personal Freedom on the other, there were thus four different political quadrants, with the Libertarians being "conservative" on economics and "liberal" on social policies, but more consistent in being pro-liberty on both. The Populists were their diagonal opposites. If you added foreign policy as a third dimension (interventionism vs. non-interventionism), you could have eight separate philosophies!

The libertarian approach is actually a convenient position for a political cartoonist. No matter whether the Democrats or the Republicans were in charge, I would have a target to criticize. While I occasionally might vote Libertarian, I never actually registered as one, because the party was never in danger of winning, enmeshed as it often was in arcane disputes over doctrinal purity rather than reaching out to a wider constituency and becoming a viable force.

In the 1980s I followed the "supply-side" economists' battle with the Keynesians with interest and became a devotee of the *Wall Street Journal*'s editorial page under Robert Bartley's editorship. I was actually pretty tough on Ronald Reagan in many of my cartoons, but I came to appreciate the dramatic changes he brought both in domestic and foreign policies from his predecessor, cutting taxes to help stimulate the economy and end "stagflation" and taking a tougher line with the Soviet Union to hasten the fall of the Iron Curtain. Other influences were Charles Murray's *Losing Ground*, which sharpened my awareness of the sometimes perverse outcomes of well-meaning social-welfare policies, and the 1983 "Nation at Risk" report about a "rising tide of mediocrity" in American schools, which increased my skepticism about various educational policy "reforms" and about the wisdom of relying on increased spending to improve education.

In the end, my political outlook would probably be best described as "classical liberal," that is, the original liberalism of limited government designed to secure individual liberties as embodied in the Constitution, rather than the big-government liberalism of the progressive movement. If the State is a "monopoly on the legitimate use of force," in the words of Max Weber, then I remain suspicious of any expansion and misuse of that monopoly, and ever mindful of the Law of Unintended Consequences. Here is a cartoon from 1986 that somewhat puckishly expresses that idea.

9. Anatomy of a Cartoon

Finally, another frequent question I get is, "How long does it take you to draw a cartoon?" In my case the answer is: longer than it should. I'm somewhat jealous of some of my cartoonist friends who seem to be able to dash out a finished cartoon in an hour, or two or three in a day. My routine is more laborious. I freely admit to being a dinosaur when it comes to my tools and techniques for cartooning. I got comfortable with using brush and ink on Bristol board years ago and haven't changed much. In the 1970s and '80s, largely due to Pat Oliphant's influence, many editorial cartoonists began using Grafix board, which was a Bristol board impregnated with an invisible pattern that could be developed simply by brushing on a special chemical. This enabled the artist to quickly achieve a gray effect for a black-and-white line drawing instead of using more time-consuming methods like Zip-a-tone, which had to be cut out and burnished down. There were various patterns of dots and lines available in either a single tone (Unishade) or two tones

(Duoshade). It had been in use since the 1930s, when it was known as Craftint Singletone and Doubletone, but it was mainly employed in advertising and by a few comic-strip artists. However, I found that the chemical process tended to discolor with age, and by the mid-'90s I was back to regular Bristol board and doing shading with a pen or brush.

Grafix board was about the only modern tool I adopted, except for the felt-tip pens I use for lettering. With the advent of the digital age, a whole new universe of tools became available, but I remained firmly analog. I did get a PC for my office sometime around the turn of the century, but I never used it for creating cartoons, other than rare instances of printing out a special typeface for use in one. Instead, with the help of the internet, it became a useful tool for research (Google Images has mostly replaced my need for a picture morgue) and for, with the aid of a scanner, emailing my cartoons to the syndicate. Photoshop and other drawing programs remained a mystery, nor did I avail myself of computer laptops and tablets. Nearly all cartoonists now add digital color to their cartoons, but I never saw much point in it before I retired, since few newspapers, including the *Journal*, used color on their editorial pages at that time. That is no longer so true, as color is being used throughout the pages of many newspapers—those that survive, that is. In the last few years, on rare occasions, I've taken a colored pencil to add some spot color when absolutely needed

The actual drawing takes, on average, about three hours, but it can vary widely depending on the amount of lettering and detail. The first stage is rough sketches, done on scratch paper, which I then improve once or twice on tracing paper. These are very quick. Here I'm trying to get the lettering, the labeling, and any dialogue as simplified as possible, plus I'm deciding on the layout of the drawing. The layout is very important, as I've always considered it the counterpart of a stand-up comedian's timing: set-up, narrative, punchline. But instead of a time dimension, one is working with a visual, two-dimensional space. I learned early on from Edmund Arnold, my graphic-arts professor at Syracuse, how a reader's eye usually travels through a picture: it starts in the upper left and moves diagonally, looping counterclockwise to pick up various elements and details and ending in the lower right. So typically, as in the example on the next page, I'd try to put set-up elements, such as a sign or title indicating the context (1), on the left side or the top and arrange the characters, dialogue, and other elements in a logical progression from left to right (2), with the punchline (3) in a caption below or in a word balloon or sign on the right.

In order to preserve the looseness of the rough sketch, I would enlarge it on the office copier to use as a template for the final pencil sketch, which was done on a 14 × 17" bond pad. I used a small light box with the sketch taped down and then traced the drawing on a piece of three-ply Bristol board with pencil. The image size of my originals was usually around 12 × 9", which would be reduced and printed on the editorial page at about 7 × 5 ½". The printed cartoon has varied in size over the years, but I've always joked that I like to draw fairly large because then the mistakes will be less noticeable in the paper.

I first would do the lettering on the final drawing with an ultra-fine Sharpie, then I'd ink the pencil drawing with a #3 sable watercolor brush and India ink. Inevitably there would be a few details that need touching up, which I would do with white gouache paint. When satisfied with the finished cartoon, I would take it to the editorial-page editor for a final okay, hoping that I hadn't made any spelling mistakes, which can be tricky to correct. Once approved, the cartoon went to the back shop. Early on it was photographed and reduced to the proper size on a Velox, which was then added to the editorial page paste-up in the composing room. I would then grab an extra Velox and drive down to the FedEx office to overnight it to the syndicate in New York. When the *Journal* converted to digital make-up, the back shop (now called digital pre-press) would scan my cartoon on a large flatbed scanner, and the digital file would be inserted onto the page by the designers in the newsroom. Then all I had to do was send the cartoon to King Features in an email.

Instead of waiting a week, the syndicate clients could get cartoons the next morning.

Over the course of my career, the look of my cartoons has changed as I gained experience, worked with different tools, and was influenced by other artists. Changes in one's "style" are a common development for cartoonists. Regular readers of newspaper cartoons, particularly comic strips, have probably noticed an evolution in the way the characters are drawn. The *Peanuts* kids in 1950, when the strip began, looked much different than they did five or ten years later. Pogo and his fellow characters changed a lot from their beginning in comic books in the 1940s to their "maturity" in the 1950s.

While in college, my style was influenced by magazine gag cartoonists, such as those in the *Saturday Evening Post*. At that time I wasn't comfortable using a brush for drawing so I relied on pens, as in this Syracuse *Daily Orange* cartoon.

During my months at the *Cleveland Plain Dealer*, I did learn to use a brush, which provides more flexibility and greater variation in line width. I became quite comfortable in using brushes during my years in Denver, where I also adopted a somewhat exaggerated and goofy style in my drawings, featuring elongated noses and a certain youthful lack of subtlety, seen in this example.

"HAD THE FUNNIEST DREAM IN CLASS TODAY..."

"You heard NOTHING! Do not meddle in those things of which you are ignorant!"

This style carried over to my early years at the *Journal*, as exemplified in this cartoon about hospital cost controls.

After several years, in the early 1980s, my style gradually matured to its current appearance, as can be seen in chapters 5 and 7.

As a side note, caricatures in editorial cartoons usually go through a similar evolution. Each time a new president enters the White House, it takes several months before the nation's cartoonists settle on various caricatures that seem to work. In my own case, here are two examples of my Ronald Reagan, early and late.

"Cheer up — we're keeping our charges within the government ceilings!"

Reagan, 1980.

Reagan, 1984.

The process is one of experimenting with exaggerating and minimizing various features until one hits on the right combination that becomes easily recognized. Needless to say, we cartoonists can also be influenced by what our colleagues are coming up with. Here are two more examples, one of an early Bill Clinton and the other of a later Clinton.

Clinton, 1992.   Clinton, 1996.

Finally, here are early and late versions of President Obama.

Obama, 2006.   Obama, 2009.

10. Keep on the Funny Side

As the reader has no doubt noticed, most political cartooning is a negative medium. It works best in the attack mode. Cartoonists don't make good cheerleaders. We thrive on criticizing and holding our subjects up for ridicule. We need targets, public figures guilty of some public transgression or embarrassment. A regular supply of scandal, waste, fraud, and disaster makes our job easier. Certainly New Mexico has obliged me in that regard over the years. However, I do prefer to leaven my cartoons with a bit of humor.

While I would never claim to be well-versed in cartooning history, I feel fairly confident in saying that humor plays a larger role in political cartooning now than it did in the past. When I look at the work of some of the earlier cartoonists, Thomas Nast, for instance, "funny" isn't the first word that pops to mind; bold, dramatic, realistic, severe, grim, angry, caustic, harsh, vicious, savage, even nasty, if you will—but rarely humorous. When I was growing up I didn't have much interest in editorial cartoons. Sixty years ago they seemed mostly on the sober side, full of clichéd images, classical references, patriotic symbols, and serious sentiments. They were usually didactic and preachy. With a few exceptions, such as Jay "Ding" Darling, they didn't even look "cartoony." Even Rube Goldberg, when he did editorial cartoons, tended to adopt the illustrative style then in vogue.

Since the 1960s, though, cartoonists have injected more humor into their work. Australia's Pat Oliphant introduced the more rambunctious and satiric approach of some of the British, Canadian, and Australian cartoonists when he moved to the United States in 1964 and became a big influence on a younger generation of cartoonists. The late Jeff Mac-Nelly brought a whimsical, gentler, sometimes goofy sense of humor and caricature, still making incisive points and belying the charge that conservative cartoonists couldn't be funny. He introduced a whole new range of clever visual metaphors. Mike Peters brought a zany, loose, and exaggerated drawing style, far removed from the serious illustrators of the past.

But by the 1980s a debate arose over whether the pendulum had swung too far toward humor. In what was becoming a golden age for political cartooning, a coterie of young cartoonists was turning out a steady supply of humorous and entertaining cartoons that could be seen around the country due to expanded syndication and more reprints in national magazines. *USA Today* and the *Washington Post* had weekly roundups, as did several regional papers. Even the cartoon-averse *New York Times* had a week-in-review page on Sunday. The "Perspectives" page in *Newsweek* had three cartoons every issue, coupled with newsworthy quotes. It was a bit of an ego boost to get reprinted in these features, particularly in "Perspectives," which often seemed to favor more topical humor rather than controversial subjects. The cartoons they selected were very clever, but they were becoming more like gag cartoons rather than offering partisan or ideological commentary. Editorial cartoonists were frequently just drawing jokes about the headlines. Often they reminded me of Johnny Carson or Jay Leno monologue bits on late-night TV.

Critics were saying that many political cartoonists were no longer the artistic assassins of yore. They were content to be comedians rather than attempting serious social criticism, going for the funny bone instead of the jugular. It was difficult to tell if they were liberal or conservative. There was some suspicion that editors didn't mind encouraging this trend. Because the gag editorial cartoon was unlikely to be controversial, fewer readers would be calling up to complain.

While I had a decent share of cartoons in *Newsweek* and other cartoon roundups in the past, few were of the simply humorous kind. This cartoon, I admit, was done purely for laughs. I predicted *Newsweek* would use it, and they did.

In recent years, however, I should point out that, with the decline of newspapers and magazines and the increase in political polarization and rancor in the nation, humor at the expense of opinion in editorial cartoons is no longer such a problem. In the era of Trump and the "Resistance," the angry, partisan cartoon has made a strong comeback.

In my cartoons I have usually aimed for a middle ground, trying to amuse while still making a serious point. I think it's more effective to wrap your message in some humor. Employing a bit of comedy may help disarm the reader. If you make him laugh or even smile, maybe he'll be more receptive to your point of view, or at least not reject it out of hand. In the words of Victor Borge, "Laughter is the shortest distance between two people." Some readers, of course, will remain unmoved and insist on taking offense. So I try to keep in mind what Lou Holtz, the former Notre Dame football coach, said: "The problem with having a sense of humor is, often the people you use it on aren't in a very good mood."

So what makes something funny? I would love to know, but to date any reliable formula for creating humor has eluded me. It's easy to say WHAT is funny but not WHY it is funny. Will Rogers's contribution was, "Everything is funny, as long as it's happening to somebody else," but that might be limited to slapstick comedy. Humor in general resists easy analysis. And it's one of those things you can ruin if you try to dissect it too much—like whenever you have to explain a joke.

The only rigorous examination of humor that I've come across is Sigmund Freud's *Jokes and Their Relation to the Unconscious*. This is a rather dense work, full of German puns, anecdotes, and whatever else passed for humor in 1905 Vienna. In it Freud theorizes that laughter arises from a discharge of pent-up mental energy and repressed emotions, a catharsis from inhibitions. I would take this in a somewhat different direction and speculate that laughter arises from a discharge of energy in the brain, in the manner of a short circuit, because a joke brings together different ideas in an unexpected and surprising way. In a similar vein, Samuel Johnson called wit the "unexpected copulation of ideas."

It is this juxtaposition of seemingly unrelated thoughts that I think is one of the fundamental techniques of political cartooning. For

instance, here's a cartoon from 1981 that brings together the festering problems at the New Mexico State Penitentiary, which had just experienced a deadly riot, with the eruption of Mount St. Helens.

Cartooning is a form of shorthand. The goal is to reduce an event or issue to a simple image. Here the volcano serves as the visual metaphor.

In another example, the *Journal* reported an invasion of wild pigs that was ravaging farms, rangeland, and animal populations in eastern New Mexico. At the same time, Gov. Martinez was arguing for a more rational process for divvying up the capital outlay budget, so-called pork projects, and vetoing some of them, prompting this cartoon.

A more recent cartoon links the protests against the Keystone X pipeline in North Dakota with a *Journal* investigative report on the flood of drugs from Mexico.

These examples show how the juxtaposition of such unrelated items can generate humor and (hopefully) a laugh in the reader, while still providing some political commentary.

At the risk of violating the admonition not to delve too deeply into analyzing humor so as not to ruin it, I propose to categorize and provide examples of the many different ways the cartoonist tries to achieve that reaction of intellectual surprise that leads to laughter.

Probably the most common technique is *comparison*, where one thing is unexpectedly likened to another, as in the previous three cartoons. In the following cartoon, the federal "Fiscal Cliff" budget crisis of 2012, so-called because a series of across-the-board budget cuts was mandated to reduce the national deficit, is compared to a roller coaster. Because federal spending is so important to New Mexico, the cuts could hurt the state's economy.

I could have also used a waterfall image, but conveniently, Albuquerque has an amusement park called Cliff's.

In this next example, when Greece was in danger of defaulting on its huge debt in 2010 and had to be bailed out, making some European Union leaders think it was a mistake to allow Greece to join the Euro, a scene from ancient Greek history made a ready comparison.

Locally, the long battle over whether to continue ignoring the problem of granting New Mexico driver's licenses to undocumented immigrants invited comparison to the familiar image of the three monkeys.

Another useful cartoon technique is *contrast*, the opposite of comparison. Here we point out differences rather than similarities. In this cartoon from the 2000 election, the US map is altered to demonstrate the outsized influence of the earliest states versus the rest of the states in the presidential primaries.

This in an example of "Big and Little" contrast, showing differences in size and importance. Another cartoon of this type from 2010 highlights the difficulties encountered in getting relief to the victims of the Haiti earthquake.

A second type of contrast cartoon is "Then and Now," focusing on differences over time. This recent cartoon was occasioned by the rash of school shootings.

The fortieth anniversary of New Mexico's infamous 1980 prison riot was the subject of the next example, which actually employs both the Then and Now and the Big and Little types of contrast.

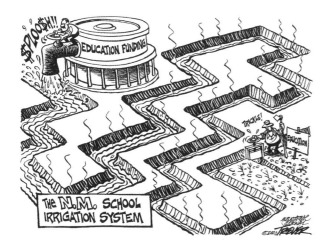

"AH—ANOTHER BOOST FOR TOURISM...."

Yet another form of contrast shows the difference between intent and result, or "Input and Output," as in this cartoon on how education appropriations get to the classroom.

A third frequent cartoonist's tool is *hyperbole*—extreme exaggeration, or carrying an idea to the point of absurdity (*reductio ad absurdum*, as they said in Rome). Of course, cartooning is pretty much exaggeration by definition. It's what we do. But the goal here is to go to ridiculous lengths in order to make a point. For instance, this cartoon from 1983, when Albuquerque had a serious pothole problem on Interstate 40 . . .

. . . stretches the truth just a mite in comparing it to the Grand Canyon.

Speaking of canyons, another example concerned the revelation of former radioactive waste-dumping into the canyons around Los Alamos, featuring a couple of huge glowing rodents outside a house.

No cartoonist can resist exaggerating a scary radiation story.

And here's one more, engaging in a bit of hyperbole (or not), poking fun at long lines at the state Motor Vehicle Department.

One of my favorite humor techniques is the classic *reversal*, where you take a phrase or concept and turn it around. This is demonstrated in this example, when the Environmental Protection Agency was blaming the coal-fired San Juan Generating Station in the Four Corners area for causing an increasing haze over the Grand Canyon. In 2012, smoke from serious forest fires in Arizona was drifting over New Mexico and affecting air quality and visibility, providing a setup for this reversal.

Another cartoon from many years ago, following the passage of California's Proposition 13, which severely limited property taxes as well as future increases, reverses the relation of hunter and bear.

"IT'S A NOTE FROM MY TEACHER...."

An old favorite is this third example, drawn when the Albuquerque public school teachers were threatening to go out on strike.

A unique province of the cartoonist—at least it used to be—is the ability to manipulate reality for effect. A classic example of this is the "altered shadow," as in this cartoon on a show of Congressional bipartisanship during the passage of the McCain-Feingold Act, which placed new restrictions on campaign contributions and spending. The shadow reflects the ongoing political battles over other issues continuing behind the scenes. This same principle applies to altered reflections in mirrors, windows, and lakes, of course. I call these *graphic tricks*, a handy cartoon device. Of course, since the advent of Photoshop and other digital programs, the photograph is now also easily subject to such alteration.

Here are two more examples of graphic manipulation, one a simple alteration of a sign . . .

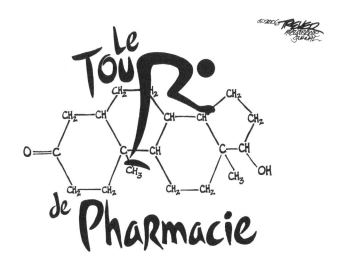

. . . the other, in the wake of yet another Tour de France doping scandal, a redesign of its logo.

Some cartoons employ a *hidden element* technique, wherein the reader can see something about to happen that the cartoon character is unaware of, such as an open manhole . . .

"WOW! LOOK AT THIS GAS COMPANY REFUND!"

. . . or the big wave in this cartoon dealing with the issue of subsidizing rebuilding in disaster-prone areas. Other images of this type are the "blind corner," with two people or cars about to collide, and the driver stopped on a railroad track with a train coming around the bend.

Next is what I call the *displaced reaction* cartoon, typified by this one on the effect of golfer Tiger Woods's knee problems on the sport . . .

. . . and the *catch-22* cartoon, here featuring two schoolkids from a poor neighborhood.

And then there's the *silver lining* cartoon, so named because of the endeavor to find the bright side of a bad situation, such as when a Senate delegation visited Greenland to check out the results of global warming.

No list of cartoon tools would be complete without that much-derided form of humor, the *pun*. It often comes in handy, as when, following Obama's economic-recovery effort that included "Cash for Clunkers" to help the auto industry, Bill Richardson came up with a plan to help the state's high-school dropouts.

And when cereal-maker General Mills built a factory in Albuquerque, a city on the route of the famous "Mother Road," it was impossible to resist doing this cartoon.

Sometimes when you haven't got a strong idea, combining a bunch of lesser ideas will do, if they're all rolled into a *kitchen sink* cartoon, like this one dealing with the problem of urban light pollution.

This by no means exhausts the inventory of cartoon humor techniques. Elements of *popular culture*—the latest movie or television show, comic superheroes, animated film characters, best-seller titles, sports incidents, even advertising campaigns—are frequently appropriated for political cartoons. Here's just one example, drawn from a popular network TV series.

And *holiday themes* are regularly seized upon by cartoonists. During the year-end holiday season, the reader has no doubt noticed a regular parade of Halloween pumpkins, witches, and vampires; Thanksgiving turkeys and pilgrims; Christmas trees, Santas, elves, and wise men; New Year's babies and resolutions. These appear in cartoons in hopes of revealing an unexpected connection to politics. Throughout the rest of the year groundhogs, leprechauns, maypoles, fireworks, and birthday piñatas are all called to cartoon duty.

Finally, I can't leave this subject without mentioning one more favorite technique—*irony*. In this case I take it to mean a cartoon with the wording saying one thing, but a picture revealing an entirely different meaning. For instance, years ago, during the infamous "Lobogate" scandal, when the Feds were investigating the UNM basketball program, we heard many fans coming to the coach's defense.

"I DON'T CARE WHAT THEY SAY ABOUT ELLENBERGER — HE PUT LOBO BASKETBALL ON THE MAP!"

YOU'VE COME A LONG WAY, BABY...

Another ironic example gives a different twist to an old cigarette slogan targeting women.

One more cartoon, on the recent border crisis and the lack of immigration reform, employs different meanings for "asylum."

All these devices in the cartoonist's toolbox are normally employed, as was noted at the beginning of the chapter, in the service of criticism, ridicule, and poking fun. But it should be noted there are some occasions when the political cartoonist puts away his weapons and behaves with more decorum. Notably, the election of a new president, governor, or mayor kicks off a "honeymoon" period, however brief, in which the cartoonist takes a *commemorative* approach, that is, simply noting the victory with a drawing, hopefully clever, that is congratulatory rather than bearing a political message. For instance,

when Ronald Reagan was first elected president in 1980, I observed the occasion with this cartoon, based on a certain ceiling in the Sistine Chapel.

(Note the crossed fingers. With stagflation, soaring interest rates, and hostages in Iran, the country was ready to take a chance on the former actor.)

Here's another example, when Vicente Fox was elected president of Mexico in 2000, ousting the long entrenched PRI party from its corrupt rule.

Another occasion calling for the commemorative approach is upon someone's death. When New Mexico Congressman Joe Skeen passed away, I drew this.

Now, the St. Peter and the Pearly Gates image is a much overused metaphor in cartoons, but I thought it particularly appropriate in this case since Skeen was notable for being one of the very few ever to have been elected to Congress as a write-in.

Sometimes taking significant elements from a subject's life makes it possible to avoid the usual cliché setting, as when former president Gerald Ford died . . .

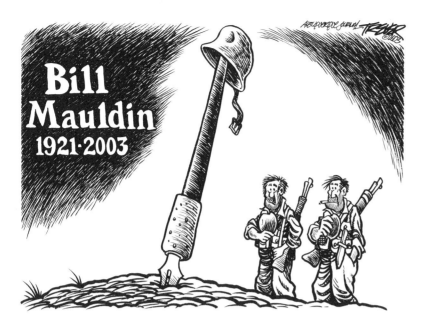

. . . I honored him for restoring respectability to the presidency. Likewise, this cartoon, done after New Mexico native and fellow cartoonist Bill Mauldin passed away, recalled his famous World War II characters Willie and Joe.

Without giving away too many secrets, I hope this gives the reader a little insight into the craft of editorial cartooning and some of the many techniques of finding humor in politics.

11. Does Political Cartooning Have a Future?

I feel truly grateful to have had a full career in editorial cartooning with a newspaper that granted me a great degree of editorial freedom. I do worry that that is becoming less possible for my fellow political cartoonists. Does newspaper political cartooning have a future? That depends, obviously, on the future of newspapers, and that prognosis is not good. Newspapers and their staffs, including cartoonists, have been in rapid decline since the 1990s. The roster of editorial cartoonists in full-time positions with benefits has been drastically thinned. Many of my friends and colleagues around the country have been terminated, laid off, or had to take buyouts and early retirements. That really came home to me when our sister paper, the *Albuquerque Tribune*, closed in 2008. On that sad occasion I drew this:

The Scripps-Howard logo and slogan underscore the importance of good journalism to our civic life, and to my profession in particular, because without the journalists writing the stories and reporting the facts that I rely on, I couldn't do my job properly. I guess I'm lucky that the *Journal* is a locally owned paper and not subject to the large media chains' obsession with the

bottom line and cutting costs and personnel. But we've not been immune from these trends either, and our newsroom is less populated these days too.

Journalism as a whole is undergoing a challenging period, beset by charges of media bias, "fake news," partisanship, agenda-driven "narratives," double standards, and worse. Gallup reports that Americans' "trust and confidence in the mass media" has been steadily sliding in this century, hitting a new low of 32 percent in 2016. In 2018 Gallup found that 62 percent of US adults think the news they read, see, and hear is biased, and nearly 40 percent say it's "misinformation." The current polarization of the country, partly driven by these media failings that also exacerbate it, isn't helping. In confirmation of this, surveys found that Democrats think most major media outlets are accurate (except for Fox and Breitbart News), while Republicans see them as biased (except for Fox News and the *Wall Street Journal*).

Some may say it ill behooves a cartoonist to complain about media bias, since their work is almost always one-sided, distorted, and sometimes malicious. Admittedly true, and it reminds me of an older survey from the 1990s, in which a *Time* magazine cover story detailed some major complaints about the press. People said the media were (1) biased and lacking balance (either too liberal or too conservative); (2) elitist and unpatriotic, not sharing in mainstream American values, eager to focus on the shortcomings of America; (3) too negative and adversarial, always looking for the bad news; (4) producing exaggerated and overblown coverage, even fabricated stories; and (5) arrogant and rude to both public officials and private citizens. When I looked at the list—biased, unpatriotic, negative, distorted, rude—I realized it sounded like a "help wanted" ad for a political cartoonist! That's my job description. Paradoxically, what the people seem to hate about the media is what they often expect from their favorite cartoonist.

The high-water mark for trust and confidence in the media was 72 percent in 1976, according to Gallup, following the acclaim journalists received for coverage of Vietnam and Watergate. Apparently, instead of being "ink-stained wretches," journalists suddenly were celebrities and being portrayed in Hollywood productions. Young journalists aspired to be the next Woodward and Bernstein, to be players and "make a difference," and that has contributed to the rise of advocacy journalism, agenda-driven coverage, and perceptions of bias. But I've always felt that making a difference is supposed to be the job of the voters in our democracy, and the job of the journalist should be to provide the voters with the objective and thorough information they need.

I think Ernie Pyle, the famed World War II correspondent who adopted New Mexico as his home, was one such journalist, trying to provide his readers with the reality of war in the trenches. There was a national Ernie Pyle Day a few years ago, which I celebrated thusly.

As for the internet, which is largely responsible for the decline of newspapers, I am mindful of the ideas of Joseph Schumpeter, which I encountered in college. Our industry is undergoing its own period of "creative destruction," which characterizes the free-market economy, and new entrepreneurs and new technologies will determine the future of the news business. I'm barely conversant with the internet and all that goes on in it, but there seems to be no lack of cartoons, including political cartoons, on the web. Creating and disseminating cartoons has never been easier or faster. Apparently, the problem is how to make a living at it, since most everyone has gotten used to thinking the internet should be free. You get what you pay for, it's said, so maybe that's why so much of what passes for information on the internet is worthless. But providing useful content takes work, which should be paid. Good journalism, including graphic commentary, has value that deserves to be compensated. Maybe someday, long after I'm gone, someone, somewhere will devise a technology, a platform, and a business plan that will attract a customer base that rewards reliable information and commentary. I hope cartooning will be a part of it.